ORIGAMI FOR KIDS

Easy Japanese Origami Instruction Book for Kids

Table of Contents

Introduction

Congratulations on purchasing *Origami For Kids: Easy Japanese Origami Instruction Book for Kids!*

You'll quickly find this is the best, easiest-to-understand introduction to the ancient Japanese art of paper folding.

There are lots of books on origami. If you visit a bookstore or search online, you'll find hundreds of them—maybe even thousands! But this book is different. This book was written with *you* in mind: you want to know about origami—what it is, where it came from, and how to do it—but you find most of the books on this subject confusing and hard to understand (and maybe even a little boring). But this book will take you by the hand and lead you step by step through 14 different origami patterns. Each pattern has helpful pictures and clear instructions to guide you. You won't be alone, and you won't get lost.

The first ones are *super*-easy. You'll be amazed how quickly you learn to fold simple, square pieces of paper into things that everybody will recognize: cats, boats, birds—even a dinosaur! As you make your way through the book, the patterns will become more challenging and you'll learn new techniques. By the time you finish *Origami For Kids: Easy Japanese Origami Instruction Book for Kids*, you'll not only be impressing your family and friends with your new-found paper-folding skills, but you'll also be amazing them with your knowledge of Japanese culture and history. You'll not only learn Japanese words, you'll learn how to draw a few of them in the Japanese language. And along the way, you'll discover things you never knew about foxes, peacocks, and many other creatures that have a connection to Japanese culture.

Let's turn the page, then, and travel back in time. We're about to find ourselves 400 years in the past, in Edo, Japan…

Chapter One: What Is Origami?

Before we start looking at origami patterns and folding paper, we need to learn what origami is and where it came from.

We live in a big, beautiful, round world that's full of people who speak different languages and enjoy different customs. Every once in a while, though, a custom from one country becomes very popular in *every* country. That's what happened with origami.

The word *origami* is a Japanese word that means "folding paper." Did you know that paper was invented over 2,000 years ago? We're so used to having paper in our lives every day that we can't imagine a world without it. But paper hasn't always existed. Instead of writing on paper, people would write on other things, like big stone tablets or even dried animal skins. In China and other parts of Asia, people would write on bamboo. But just over 2,000 years ago, a Chinese man named Cai Lun invented paper—or something very close to it. Hundreds of years later, another Chinese man, Ts'ai Lun, invented a type of paper that was much closer to the kind of paper we use today.

Legend has it that, one day, Ts'ai Lun watched a wasp making its nest by chewing up pieces of bamboo, mixing them with its own saliva and then working the whole mess into a flat sheet with its feet. The wasp then used the sheet to build a wall in its nest. Ts'ai Lun copied the wasp, making a paste of bamboo and water and spreading the flat sheet to dry in the sun. Knowledge of his work spread slowly, first to the Middle East, and then, much later, into Europe.

Origami first became really popular in the Japanese city of Edo, which today is called Tokyo and is the capital of Japan. Paper was expensive and not available to most people. Paper and paper folding was limited to religious rituals and formal ceremonies. But over time, as paper became cheaper to make, the people in Edo began to have fun folding paper into shapes that looked like animals, flowers, and insects. They called this art *origami*—"folding paper"—and it quickly became very popular. People would make origami butterflies and use them as wedding decorations. They would attach origami to gifts, like we do today with greeting cards. Instead of a card, people would receive an origami bird or flower.

The idea is really very simple: take a flat, square sheet of paper and make it into a kind of sculpture by folding and bending it in creative ways. There are only a small number of basic origami folds, but the amazing thing about origami is that the folds can be combined in a lot of different ways to make really beautiful designs. The best-known origami design is the Japanese crane, which is a pretty bird very common in Asia. And guess what? You're going to learn how to make an origami crane! You will follow a pattern that is 400 years old!

Origami's Influence

It is easy to make the mistake of thinking that origami is simply a pastime, or even something silly. Because the truth is, origami has had a significant impact on how our technology has helped us. Would you believe that origami has influenced how we build cars? It has! Think of the airbags in the steering wheel and dashboard of your family's car. How did people ever figure out how to stuff such big airbags into those little spaces? That's right: they studied origami. And have you ever seen those huge mirrors and solar panels on space stations? How did the astronauts ever figure out how to get those huge things into such small spaceships? Yes, that's right: they studied the principles of origami.

Origami has had an influence on:

- How we build cars

- How we build microscopes

- How we do heart surgery

- How we build robots

Origami isn't just fun, it can actually help us. Doing origami on a regular basis has been proven to help students become more focused, coordinated, and better at math.

But most of all, making origami is just plain fun.

So what does it take to do it?

Origami designs begin with a square sheet of paper. It can just be plain white paper, it can be colored, or it can even have different colors, prints, and patterns on each side. It's up to you, whatever you want. You can use a small square piece of paper or a big one. Again, it's up to you. Be creative!

People sometimes use scissors when doing origami, but a lot of people prefer to simply fold their paper and not use any other tools. That's what we'll be doing in this book. You won't have to use scissors for any of the patterns you see.

Before we move on to the next chapter, I want to show you something that's pretty cool:

Do you know what that is? That's the word *origami* in traditional Japanese letters. You might want to take some time and learn how to draw it. Then you can show your friends that you not only know how to make origami, you also know how to write it in Japanese!

Chapter Two: Getting Started

Thankfully, you don't need many supplies to practice origami. In fact, you should be able to find most of it around your home. It is this simplicity that makes origami such an enjoyable craft—you can make it from almost any paper and you can do it almost anywhere: on the school bus, at the library, or even camping in a tent. If you have paper with you, there's an excellent chance you can make some origami with it.

Some people think that you need expensive and hard-to-come-by origami paper, a guillotine to cut it with, and something called a "bone folder," which helps make sharp folds and creases. It's called a bone folder because it is traditionally made from a bone, but today, most of them are plastic. You really don't need any of these things, especially when you're just starting out. All you need is a piece of paper and the ability to use your hands.

Of these things, the most likely for you to think you need is origami paper. However, you do not really need special paper any more than other special tools. I recommend starting with only the paper you need, and as your interest and skill expands, you can invest in more. If all you have nearby is a notepad, then use that. If all you have is a newspaper, use that. For simple folds, copy paper works very well. It keeps a crease, doesn't easily wrinkle, and, best of all, you can find it pretty much everywhere. The only requirement is that the paper needs to be square. That means that if you use, for example, a piece of notebook paper, you'll need to cut or tear it into a square.

There is special paper that's already made for origami called *kami*, which is the Japanese word for paper. It's usually colored on one side and white on the other, but sometimes it has bright colors on both sides. Kami is usually inexpensive and is very good for beginners. It holds a crease very well (which is important in origami, as you will soon see); it's not expensive; and it comes in lots of colors.

There is also another type of origami paper called *tant*. It is stiffer than kami and comes in bigger sizes. But it also tears easily, and only comes in solid colors. This means that kami is probably the best choice for beginners. I recommend that you visit a craft or arts supply store; you'll find lots of different paper made just for origami and can choose what's best for you.

Other Supplies?

You won't need scissors for any of the patterns in this book. What you *might* want, however, are some magic markers. For example, in this book you'll be making an origami cat face, and you can make it extra cute by drawing some whiskers on it with a magic marker. And if you want to make it extra *extra* cute, you can get a pack of googly eyes at the craft store when you buy your paper.

Take a look at the origami cat face you're going to make in this book:

If you're very artistic and want to have some fun, you can draw those eyes on your cat face yourself. But if you prefer, you can get a pack of googly eyes at the craft store and stick them to your origami. The googly eyes will shake and roll around and make your cat look funny and alert. Some of the googly eyes you can buy in the craft store have sticky backs; some don't. Just in case your googly eyes don't already have glue on them, you might also want to get a glue stick while you're at the craft store.

Checklist

What do you need to start? Here's a handy checklist:

- Square paper

- Magic markers (optional)

- Googly eyes (optional)

- Glue stick (optional)

- Enthusiasm (this is the most important requirement!)

Once you have everything you need, turn the page and learn how to read the symbols you'll see in the patterns. (Don't worry, there are only a few and they're easy to remember.)

We're almost there…

Chapter Three: Symbols

This book has lots of pictures to help you make origami. The pictures are clear and are sometimes all you will need to complete the project. The written instructions are easy to follow, too. But the pictures do contain some symbols that you might be seeing for the first time, so I want to make sure you understand what they mean.

Take a look at this picture:

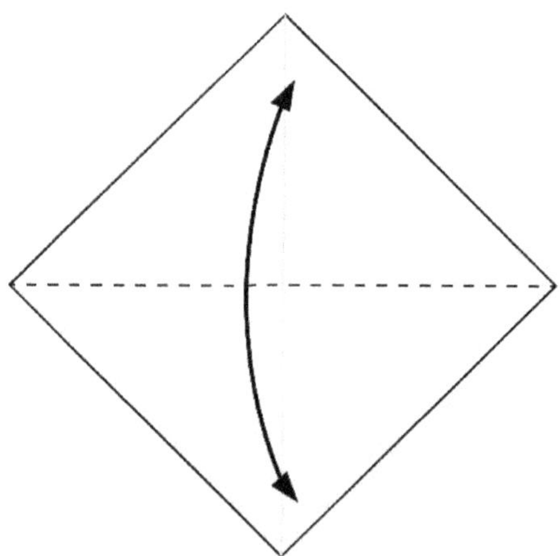

The dotted line shows you where you should fold and unfold.

The arrows show you the direction to fold the paper.

The solid gray line shows you where the crease should be.

Now take a look at this picture:

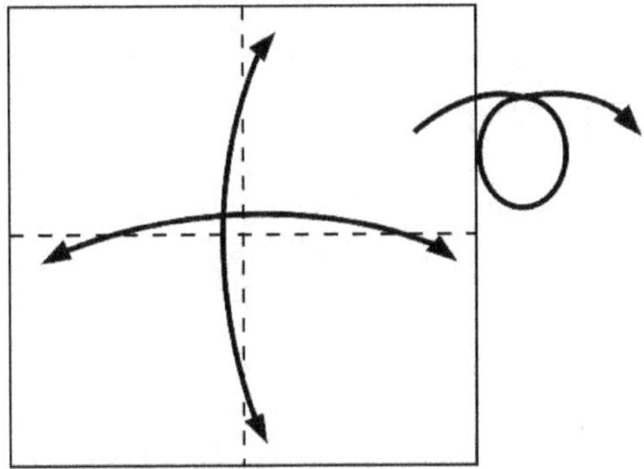

If you see an arrow that loops, it means you should turn the paper over.

And that's it! (See? I told you they were easy to remember.)

Don't worry if you forget them. The instructions for each pattern are easy to understand, and I'll refresh your memory along the way.

But if you ever need to study them, the symbol pictures will always be here in Chapter Three for you to study.

Time to Begin!

Are you ready? You're about to start a journey and learn an ancient art. You now have everything you need. There's no need to wait any longer—let's go!

Chapter Four: An Easy Heart

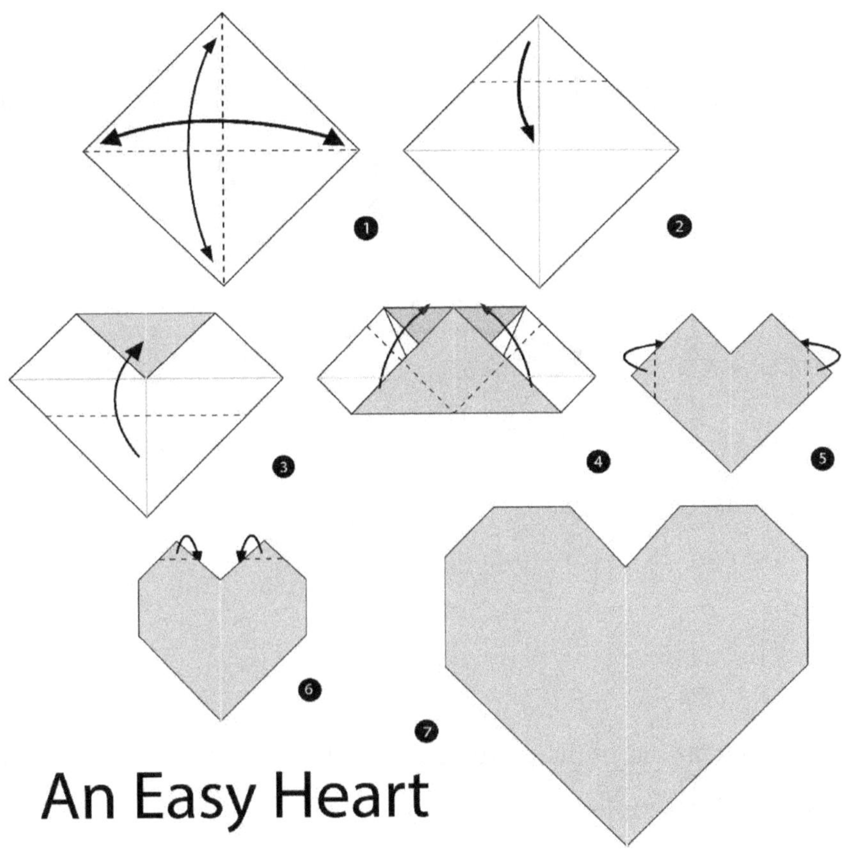

Alright, let's get going with something easy, but also exciting and beautiful: a heart!

This origami needs only a few basic folds and is a good introduction to the step-by-step method of this book.

Step 1

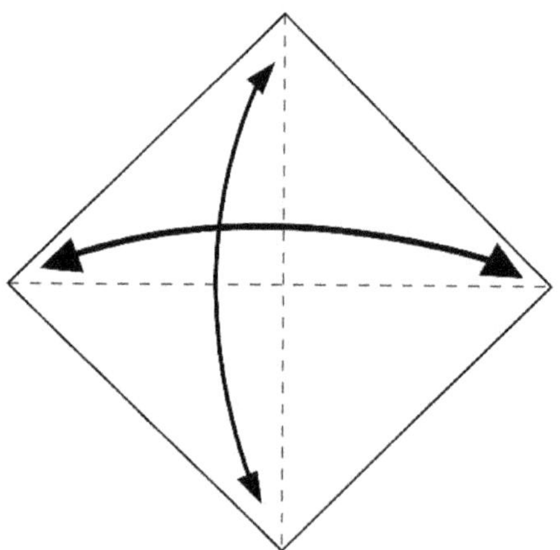

As you can see in the picture, **Step 1** is very easy. All you have to do is make two simple folds.

Fold #1: Take two opposite corners and fold the square piece of paper in half; then unfold the paper.

Fold #2: Take the *other* two opposite corners and fold the paper in half again; and again, unfold the paper.

Congratulations! You've just taken your first step into the world of origami!

Step 2

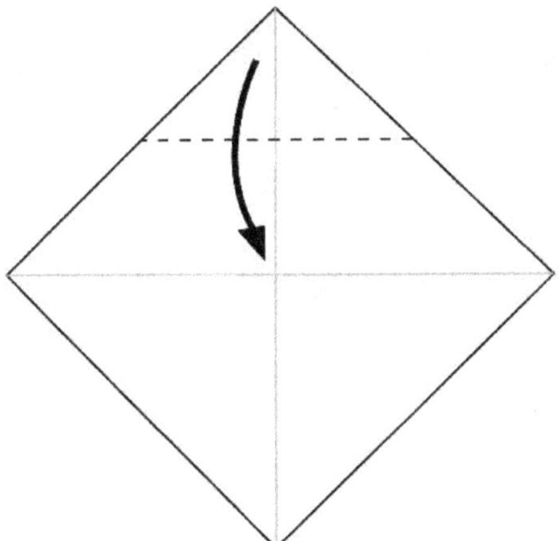

Place your paper flat on the table with one of the corners pointing away from you. (Do you see the solid gray lines in the picture? You should have creases in your paper where the gray lines are.)

Now, fold that corner down so that its point touches the center of the paper. See? Just like in the picture.

Step 3

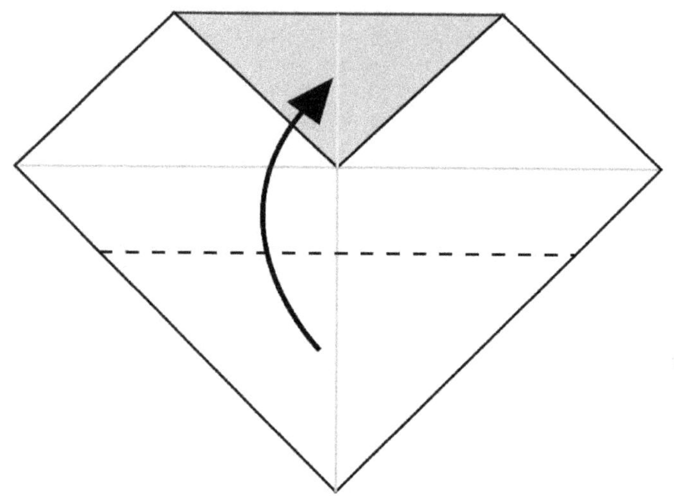

Now you're going to take the point of the *bottom* corner and bring it up so that it touches the very top of the fold you just made. Don't stop at the center of the square but go all the way to the other side. Once the bottom corner is even with the other side, make a fold.

Step 4

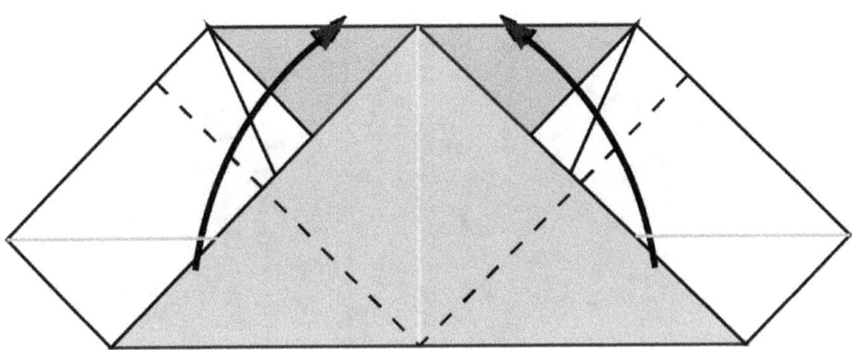

This step might look complicated, but it's actually very simple. You're going to make two diagonal folds here—one on the left and one on the right. Fold each side up toward the center and top of the paper. Follow the picture and it'll be perfect.

(Remember: the solid gray lines show you where the creases are. The dotted black lines show you where you should fold.)

Step 5

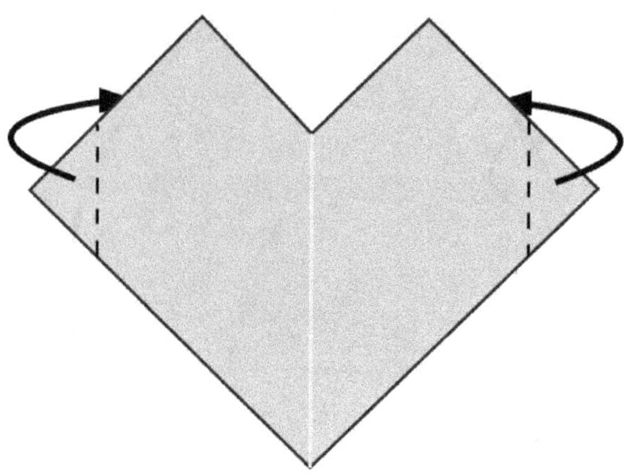

You're getting closer! Your paper should now look a little like the letter V.

Take the point of each side—again, on the left and the right—and fold just a little bit of it back. Do you see the arrows in the picture? They show you which direction to make the folds. In this step, for example, you need to fold the corners back and behind the heart.

Step 6

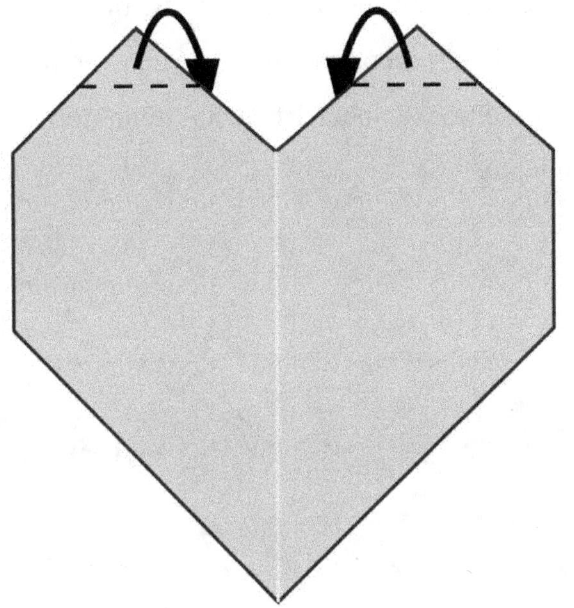

Now do the same thing to the two points at the top of the paper: fold them behind the heart.

Congratulations! You did it!

Give yourself a pat on the back. You just made your first origami figure, which is quite an accomplishment. And even better, you made a *heart*. Give it to someone special to you—then come right back and start the next chapter!

Chapter Five: A Cup

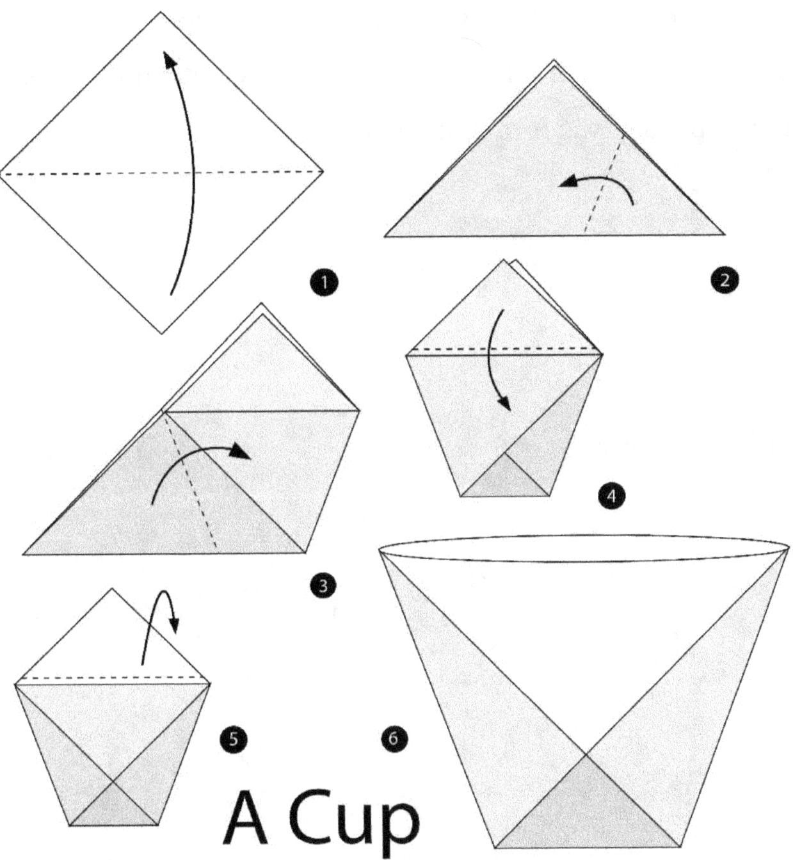

A heart is beautiful. But a cup?

Yes, an origami cup can be beautiful, especially with colorful paper. But even with plain paper, an origami cup can be interesting and fun to make. Just follow the simple instructions and in a matter of minutes, you'll be holding in your hand a cute little paper cup. I wouldn't put any water in it, though!

Step 1

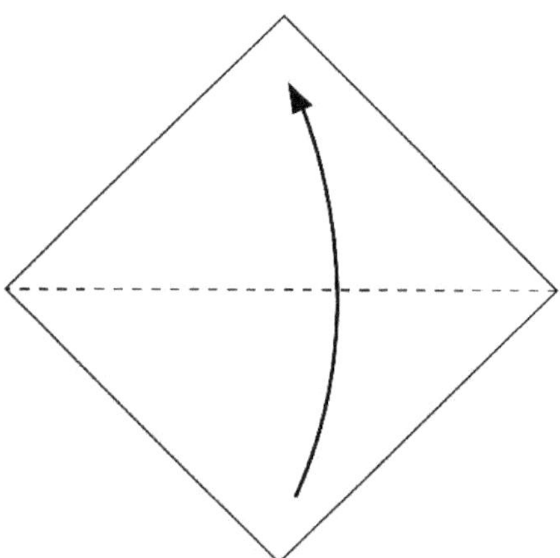

Just like you did with the origami heart, start with the square paper flat on the table. One of the corners should be point   vay from you.

By now you know what the dotted line means: it shows you where to make the fold. As you can see in the picture, you need to take the bottom corner (the one that's facing you) and bring it even with the top corner (the one that's facing away from you) and fold the paper in half right there.

Got it? Great! You just completed **Step 1**.

Step 2

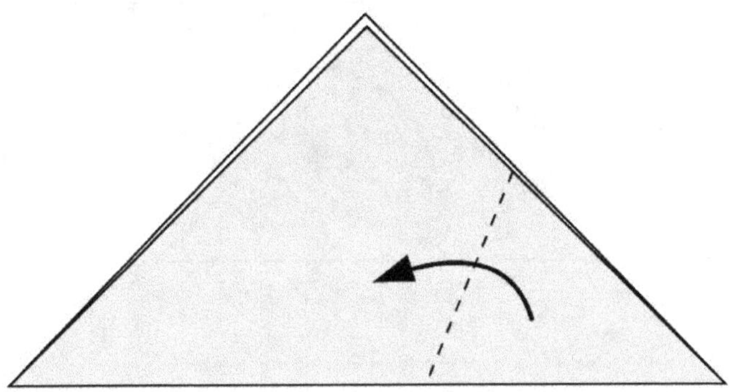

The paper should still be folded in half, with the points facing away from you.

Now take the right corner and fold it along the dotted line you see in the picture. The point of the right corner should now be touching the other side of the triangle, almost halfway down.

Step 3

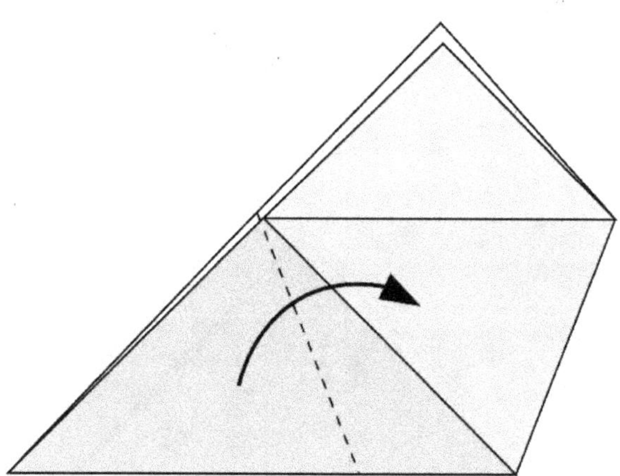

In **Step 3** you're going to do the same thing you did in **Step 2**, but from the other direction.

Take the left corner and fold it to the right along the dotted line you see in the picture. The point of the left corner should reach all the way to the right side. If this is confusing to you, don't worry, just look at the picture in **Step 4**. It will show you where the left corner should go, and what the figure should look like.

This is probably a good time to mention that if you make a mistake with your folds, it's okay. You're just beginning to learn an ancient art, so it's natural to make some mistakes along the way. If you ever fold something incorrectly, that's okay! Simply unfold it and try again. This is the time to learn and make mistakes. Very soon, you'll be making elaborate and artistic designs like people did 400 years ago in Japan.

Step 4

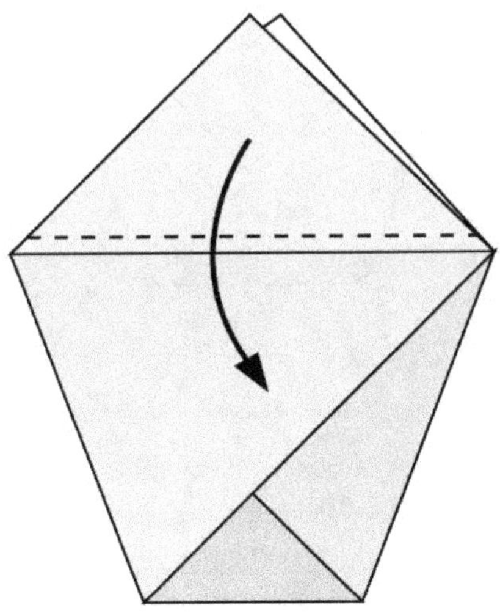

You now should have two flaps pointing up at the top of your cup. Take the flap that's closest to you and fold it downward along the dotted line you see in the picture. You'll notice that your earlier folds have made a little "pocket" along the inside of the cup. Tuck the flap closest to you into that little pocket.

Step 5

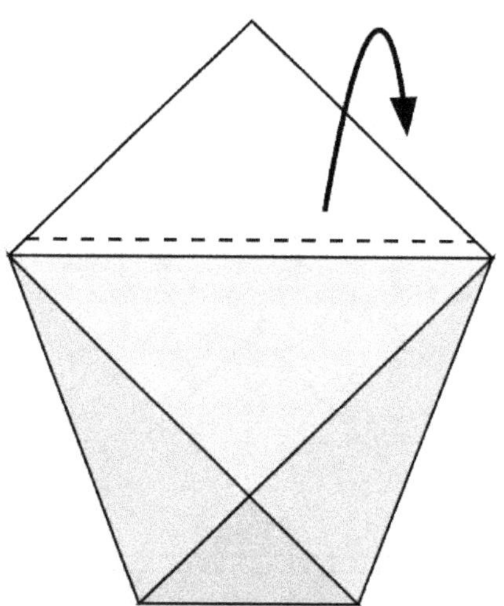

You now have one flap left.

Fold it downward like you see in the picture and tuck it into the cup. If you give the cup a gentle squeeze at its sides, it will open up and…

Boom! You're Done!

Congratulations, you've just completed your *second* origami. You'll be a pro in no time!

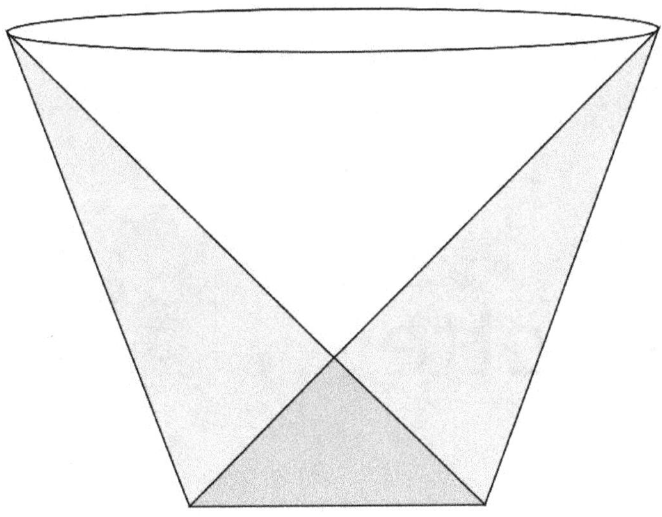

Chapter Six: A Letter

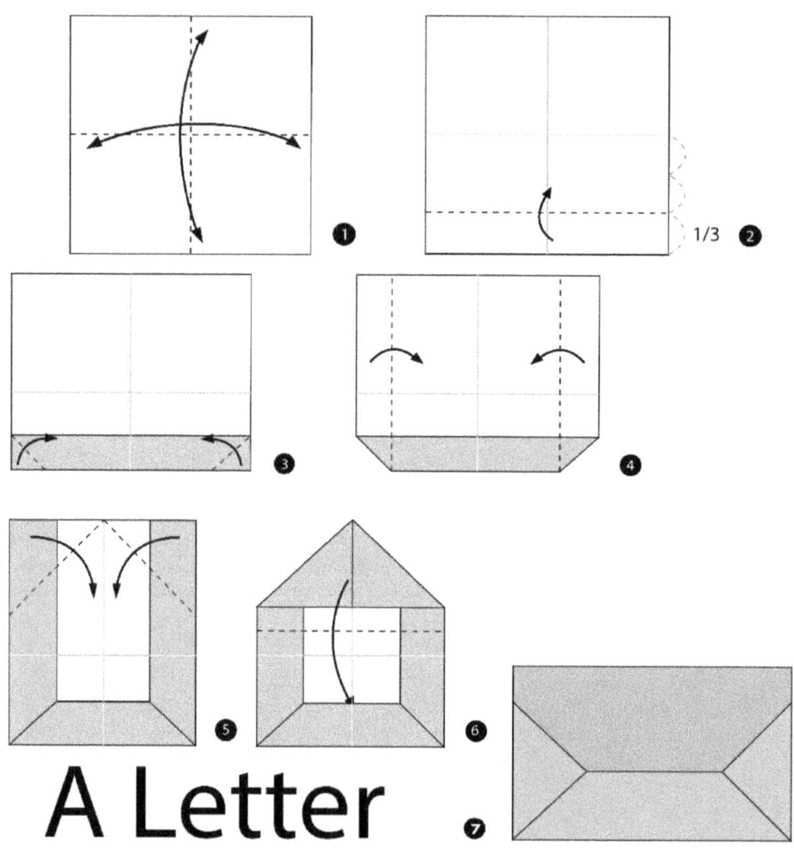

With all our technology—computers, cell phones, email—we've forgotten the joy that comes from receiving an actual handwritten letter. We text on our phones, we send many emails per day, and maybe we even have a video chat with a family member who is far away. These are all great things. But isn't it wonderful to know that someone took the time to sit down, grab a pen or pencil, and write you a *letter*? With this origami, you'll be able to give that joy to someone. And guess what? You won't even need to find an envelope to mail your letter—because, as you'll soon see, your letter *is* the envelope!

Step 1

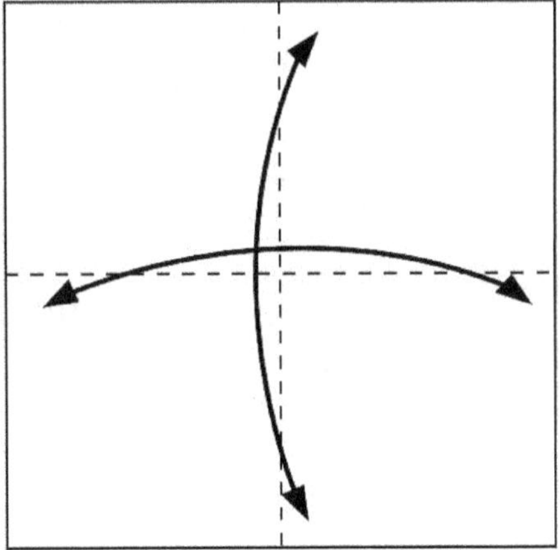

Lay your paper flat on the table in front of you. Make sure that none of the corners are pointing towards you or away from you. You want the paper to be positioned just like it is in the picture.

Now fold the paper along the dotted lines you see in the drawing. You will make two folds. The first will be up and down: take the top side of the square and fold it toward you until it is even with the bottom side. Now do the same thing again, only this time from side to side.

Step 2

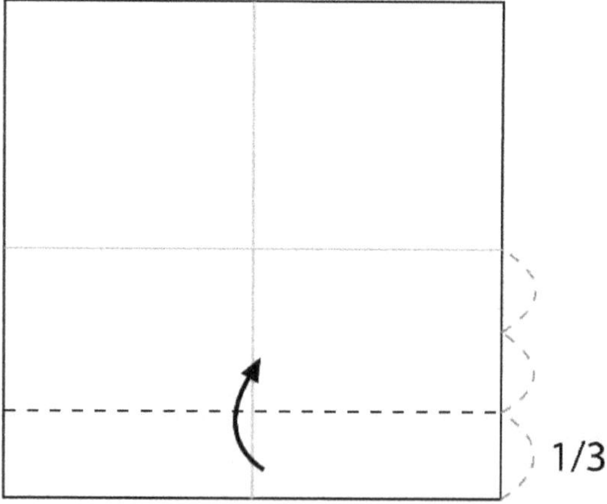

In this step, you're going to take the bottom edge of the square and fold it about 1/3 of the way toward the center. Imagine the bottom half of the square being divided into three pieces: now fold your paper about that much. If you look closely at the picture and fold where the dotted line is, you'll be just fine.

Again, you want to fold the bottom edge of the square 1/3 of the way toward the center.

Step 3

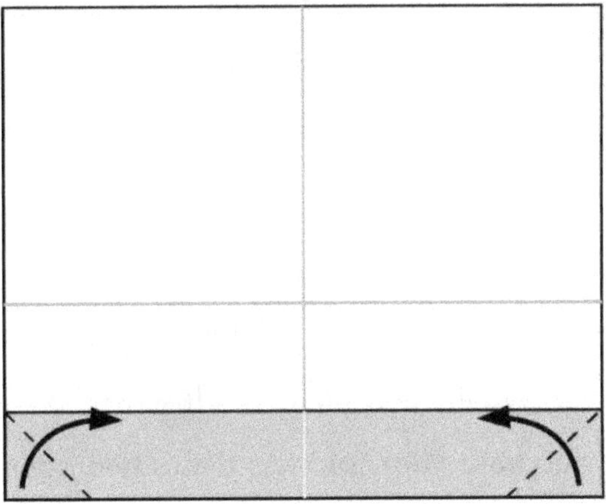

As you can see from the picture, you have already made your 1/3-fold. That's great. Now you need to fold the bottom corners inward toward the center. The dotted lines in the drawing show you where to fold. And remember, these need to be diagonal folds.

Step 4

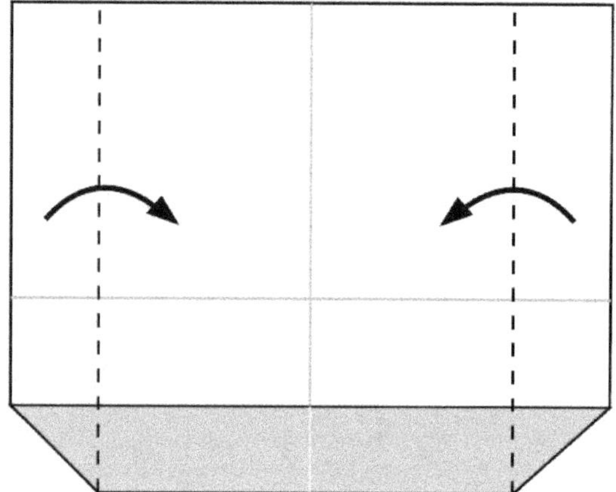

You're going to make two more folds. These will be moving from the outside in. Don't make the folds too close to the edges or too close to the center. If you base your folds on the dotted lines in the drawing, it'll be perfect. Start with the right side and then do the left. Be sure that your creases are nice and sharp. Those creases will be the sides of your envelope.

Step 5

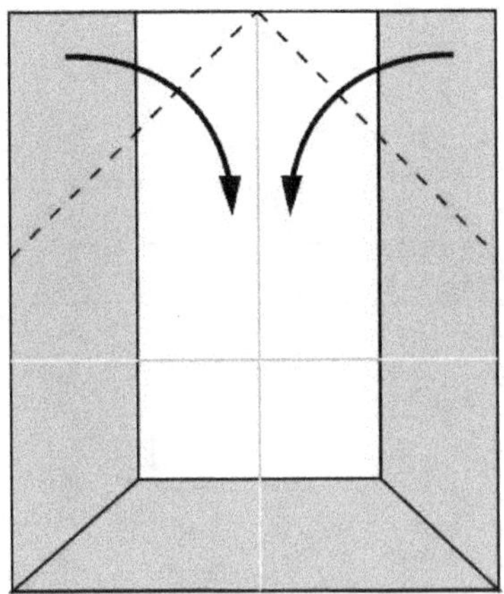

In this step you're going to take the two top corners and fold them diagonally towards the center. Study the picture and notice where the dotted lines are. Start with the top right corner and fold it along that line. Now do the same thing with the top left corner. If you make the folds correctly, then the edges of the two corners should be even with each other along the crease that runs down the center of the paper. If you need to back up and try again, that's perfectly okay. Take your time.

Step 6

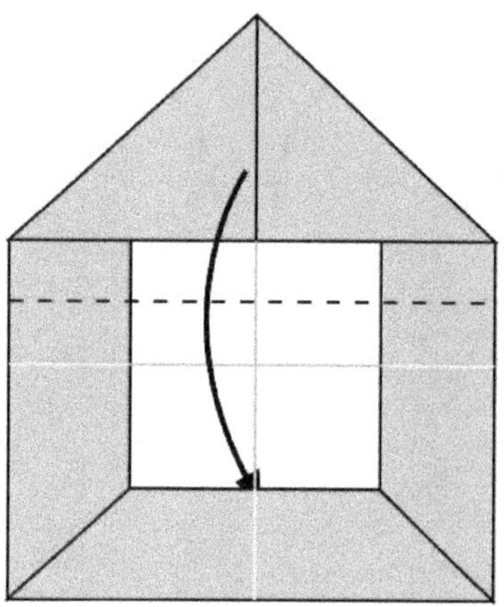

Now that your folds are correct and the top two corners have met in the center crease of the paper, you're going to fold down the top point of the paper. Notice where the dotted line is in the picture. Make your fold there.

Take another look at the picture. Do you notice how the tip of the arrow disappears behind the bottom flap of the paper? That's because when you make the fold and bring down the point, you need to take the point and tuck it behind that flap, just like the tip of the arrow.

Ready to Send! (Well, Almost...)

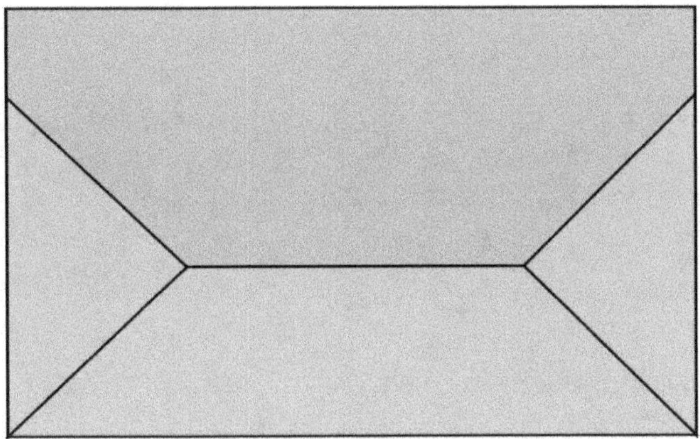

Once you tuck the top point behind the bottom flap, then you've "sealed" the envelope and you're ready to send it.

There's only one problem.

You didn't write a letter!

But that's okay. This time was just practice. Once you get comfortable making this type of origami, you'll be able to take a piece of paper, write a letter on it, and then fold it up just like you did this one. And whoever you write will be happy you did.

Chapter Seven: A Cicada

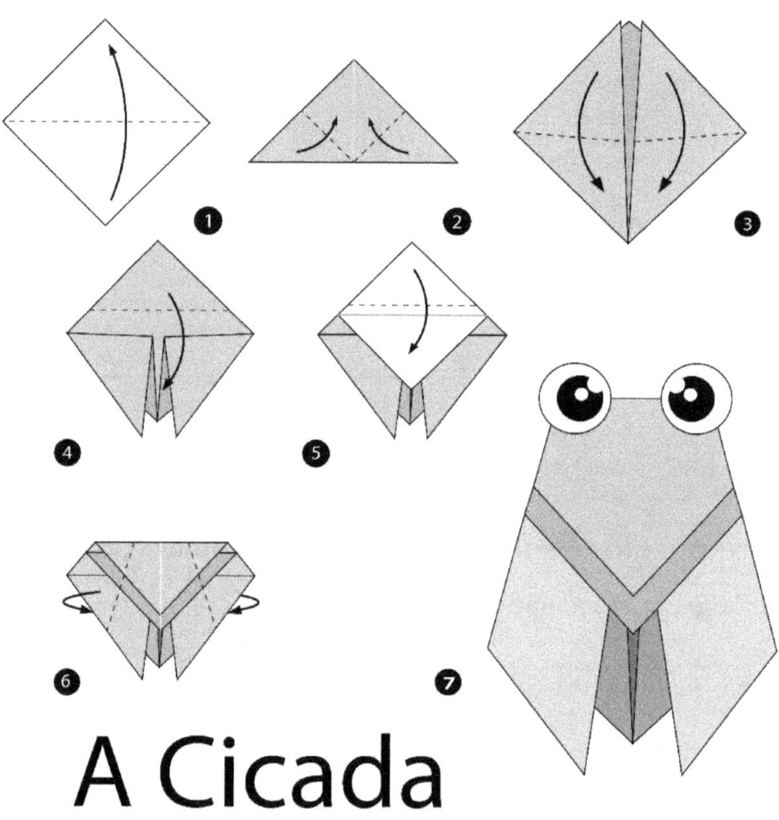

A Cicada

A cicada is a large flying insect that has a special and beloved place in Japanese culture. Do you know why? Because when they start buzzing—and they have a very loud buzz—it means that summer has arrived. So even though cicadas can be a little weird-looking, they're harmless and bring good news: Summer's here!

In Japan there are over 30 different kinds of cicada, and each has its own "song." Even though it just sounds like buzzing to most of us, the sounds made by cicadas are actually a form of communication. Some people like to listen to cicadas and try to hear the different songs.

And some people like to make cute little cicada origami!

Step 1

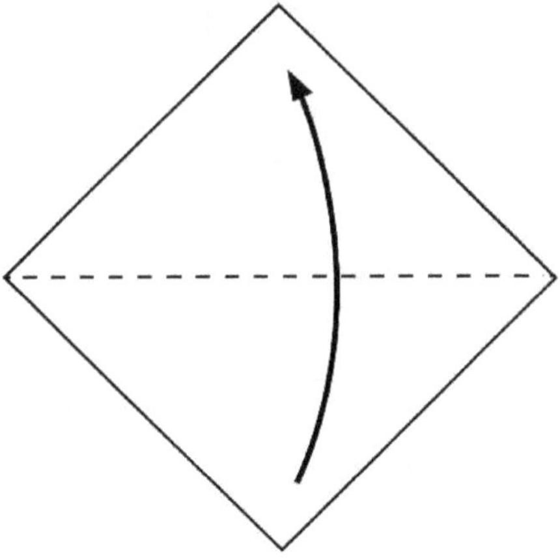

Place the square flat on the table as shown, with one corner pointing at you and one corner pointing away from you. You're going to fold the paper in half by taking the bottom corner (the one that's pointing at you) and lifting it toward the top corner (the one that's pointing away from you). Once you've made the fold, make sure you give it a good crease.

Step 2

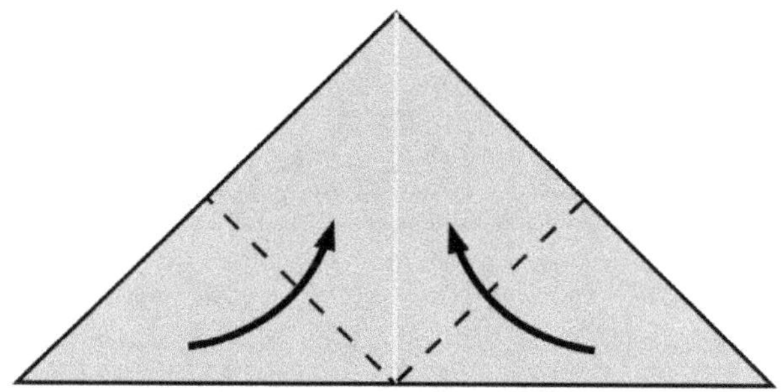

You should now have a triangle with a corner pointing away from you.

The next thing you're going to do is fold the two bottom corners toward the top. Take a look at the drawing. Notice where the dotted lines are. That's where you need to make your folds. Start with the right corner and fold it so that its edge is nearly even with the crease running down the center of the triangle (that's the solid gray line). Now do the exact same thing with the left corner.

Step 3

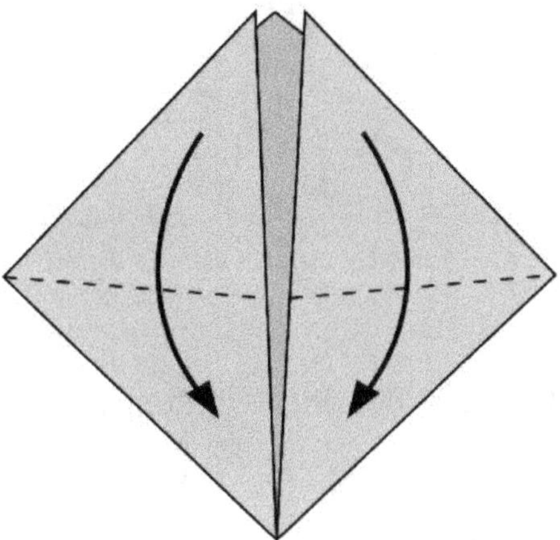

This is what your paper should look like now.

Next, you're going to take the two top flaps and fold down them along the dotted lines you see in the picture.

Step 4

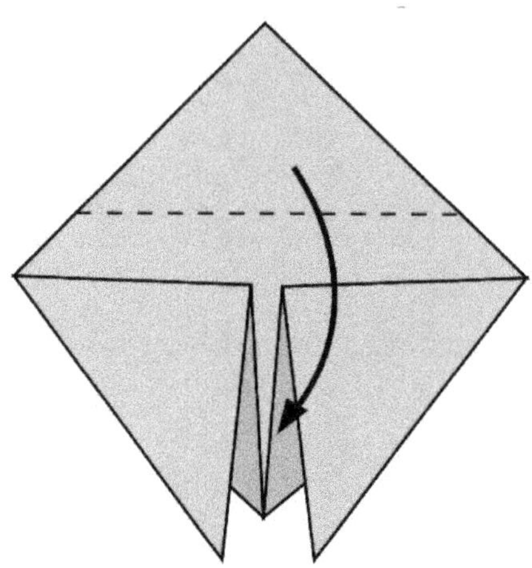

Once you've folded down the two flaps, you'll notice that there are two layers of paper pointing up. Take the layer closest to you and fold it down towards you, so that it covers parts of the two flaps you folded in **Step 3**. The dotted line in the drawing should help you know where to make the fold.

Step 5

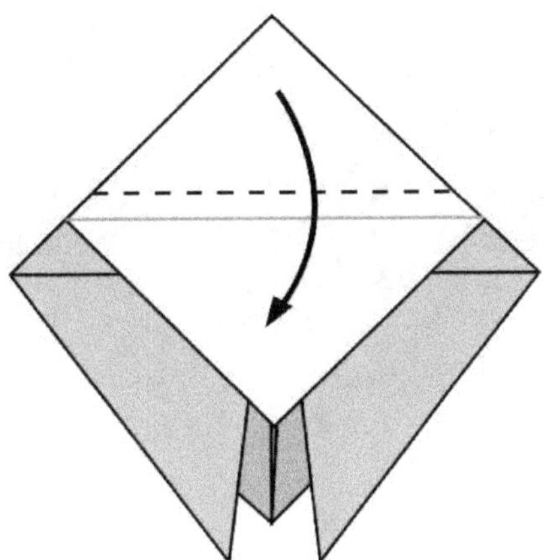

When you fold down the layer closest to you, you'll see that there's still one more layer. You will need to fold down that layer, too, but with an important difference. Notice that the dotted line in the drawing is just slightly above the previous fold. Don't make the mistake of simply folding both layers of paper over and creasing them together. You will want a slight difference in their fold lines, a slight space between the folds. If this is confusing, feel free to look ahead to the next step and study the picture. It'll give you a good idea of where the two folds should be.

Step 6

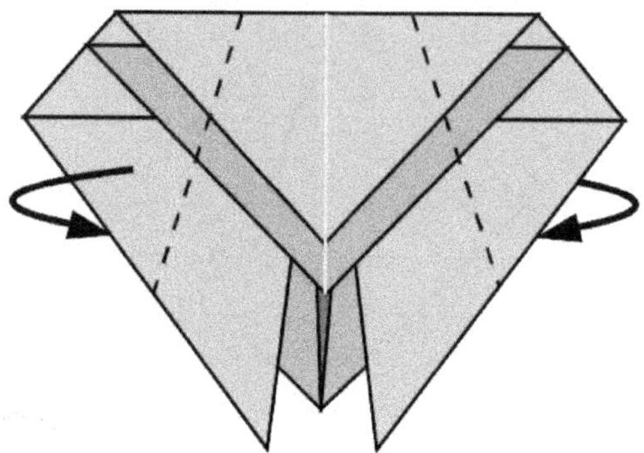

In this step, you're going to make two more folds. Starting with the right side of your paper, make a diagonal fold along the dotted lines. As you can see from the direction of the arrows in the picture, you will need to fold the paper *back* (behind the cicada) and make a good crease. Now move to the left side of the cicada and make a similar fold there. Again, you will be folding *behind* the cicada and making a firm crease.

Step 7

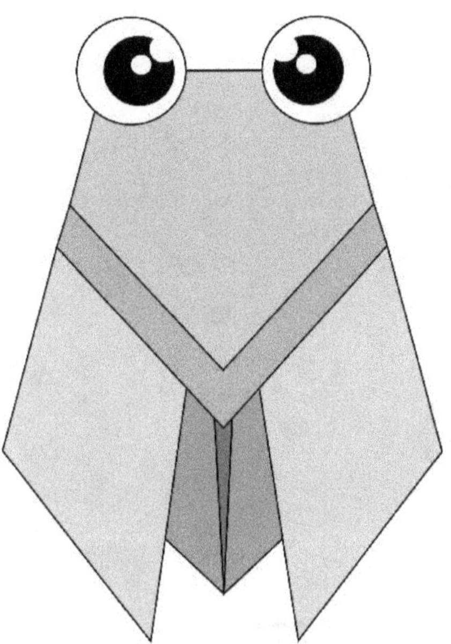

Take two plastic googly eyes and stick them on your cicada as shown in the drawing.

Ta-da!

You now have your very own pet cicada. Fortunately for you, *your* cicada doesn't do a lot of buzzing!

Chapter Eight: A Bird

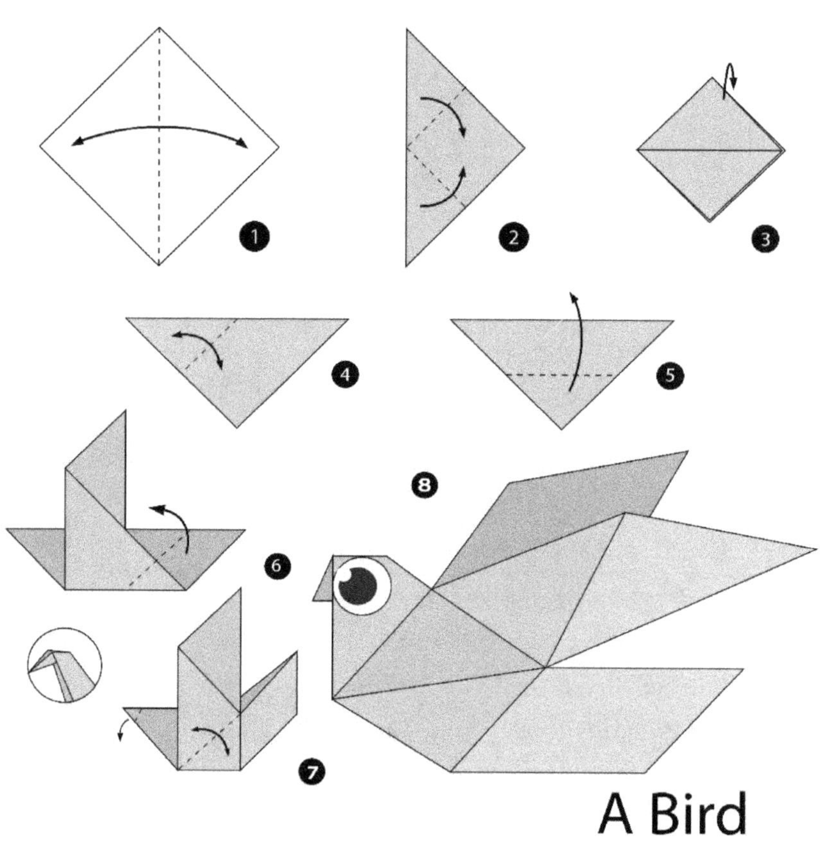

A Bird

Let's see: you made a heart, then you made a cup and a letter, and then you made an insect—now it's time to make an animal!

Animal patterns are very common in origami, and bird patterns are maybe the most popular. It's very appropriate, then, for you to have a bird as your first origami animal. You'll notice that this pattern is a little more difficult than any of the ones you've made so far. But you're learning fast and can do it!

Step 1

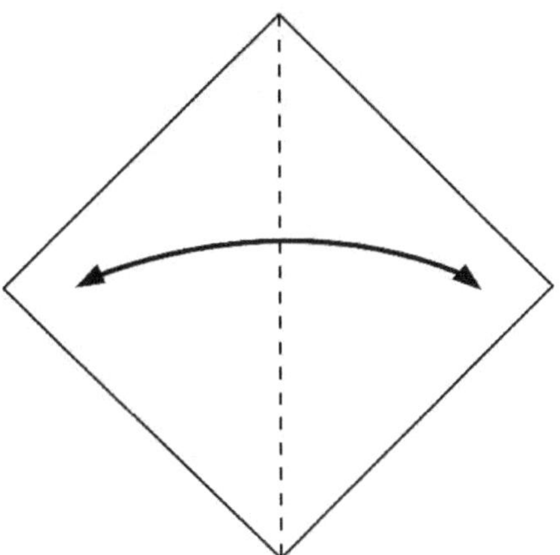

Place the paper flat on the table, with one corner facing away from you, then fold the square in half, right down the middle as shown in the picture. The left corner should be folded on top of the right corner.

Step 2

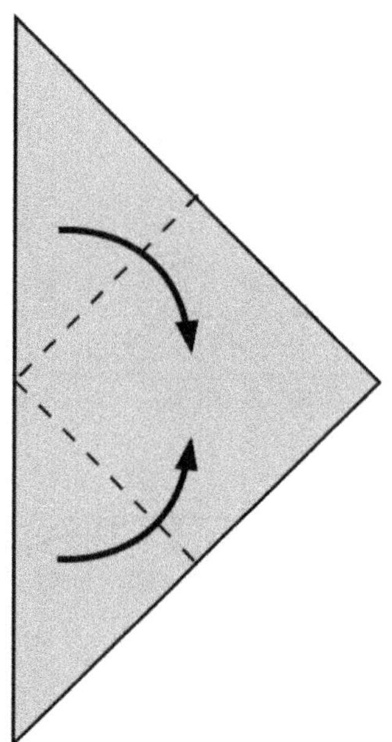

In front of you, the paper should now be a triangle pointing to the right.

Take the top corner (the one facing away from you) and fold it as shown in the picture. Once you make the fold, the point of the top corner should be lined up with the point of the corner to the right.

Now do the same thing with the bottom corner (the corner that's facing you).

When you have completed this step, both the top corner and the bottom corner should be lined up with the corner facing to the right.

Again, this may seem confusing at first. If you're unsure what things should look like after you've completed this step, simply look at the picture in **Step 3**. It will show you.

Step 3

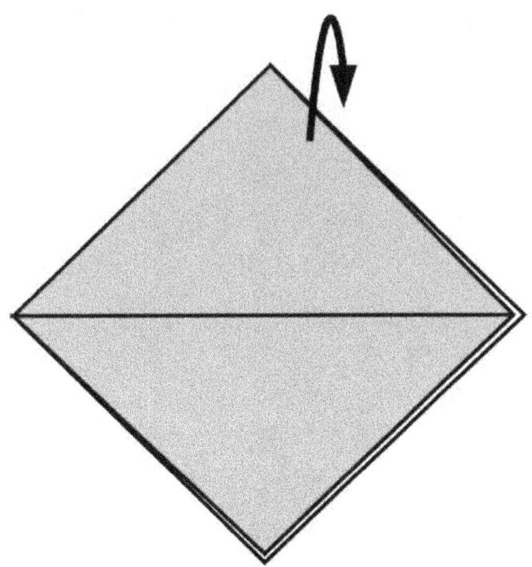

As you can tell from the arrow in the picture, you should now fold down the top half of the paper to the back. When you are done, you should have a triangle with a corner pointing towards you on the table.

Step 4

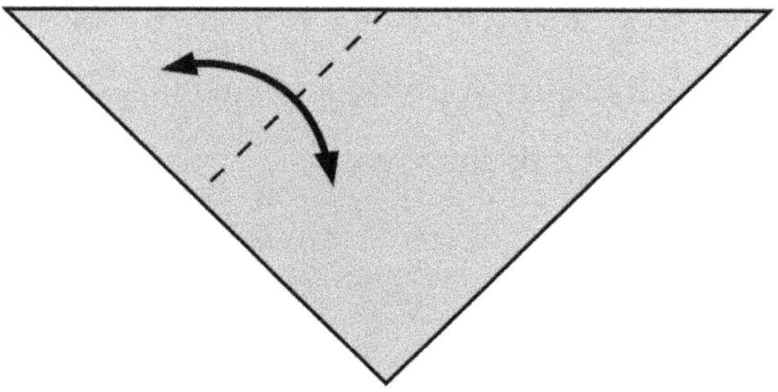

Take the left corner and fold it along the dotted line as in the picture.

Now unfold it.

Step 5

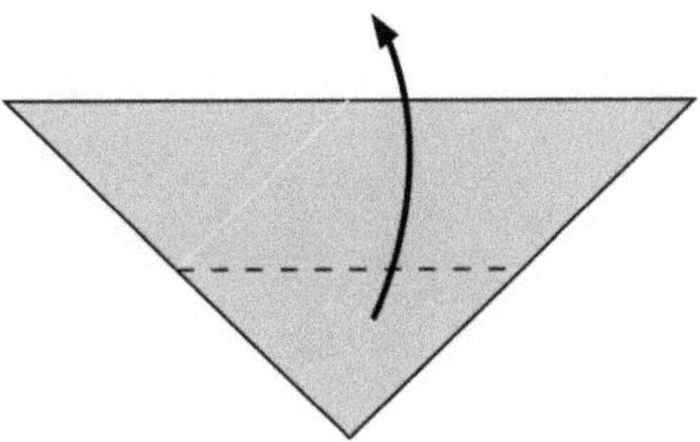

Do you see the solid gray line in the picture? Do you remember what it means? That's right: it's the crease you made in the previous step. Now fold the bottom corner up along the dotted line.

Step 6

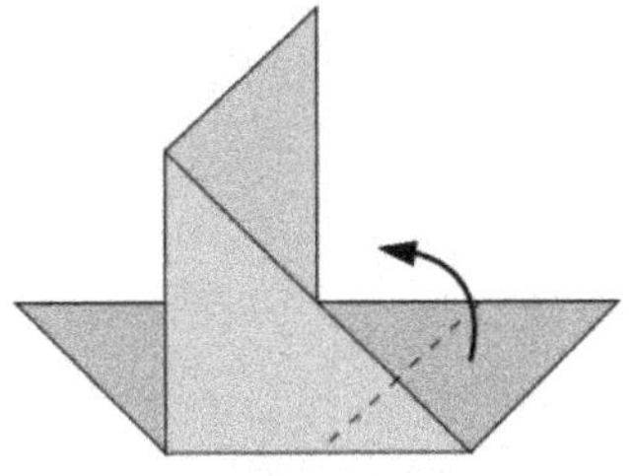

Let's create some wings!

This fold may require a couple of tries to get right, but once you do, you'll have it forever.

Open the paper slightly and fold along the dotted line you see in the picture.

Step 7

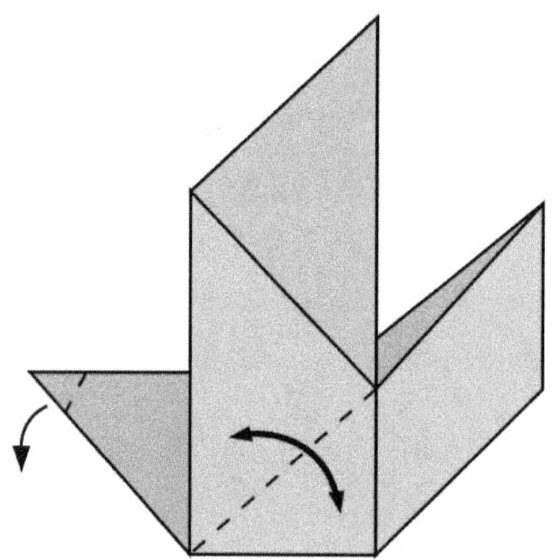

This step actually has two folds.

To make the first one, look at the double-sided arrow. A double-sided arrow means that you'll make a fold in both directions along the dotted line.

The second fold is much simpler: just follow the single-sided arrow and fold the tip of that little corner back. Congratulations! You just make a bird beak!

Step 8

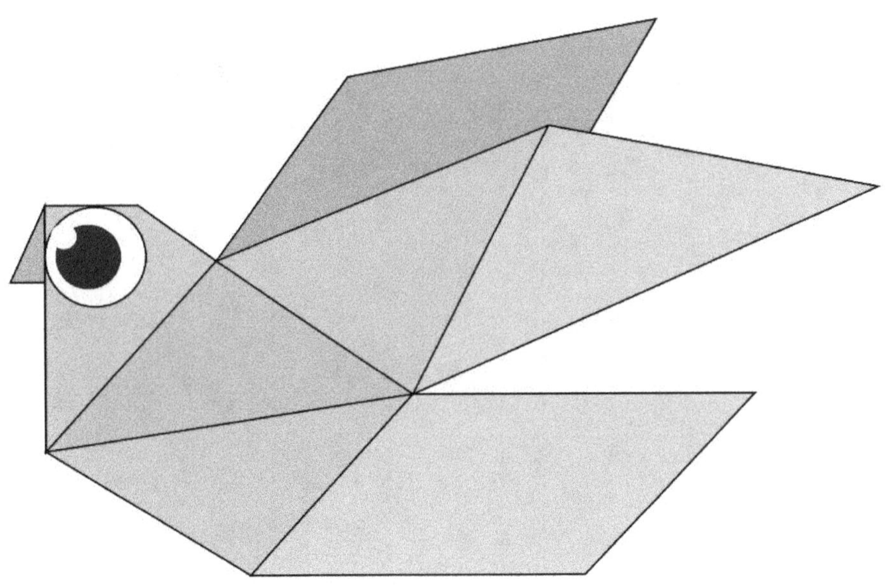

Although you don't *have* to do anything more, it's always fun to add an eye. You can either draw an eye with a magic marker, or you can stick on a googly eye from the craft supply store.

Either way, you're done! Great job!

Chapter Nine: A Little Boat

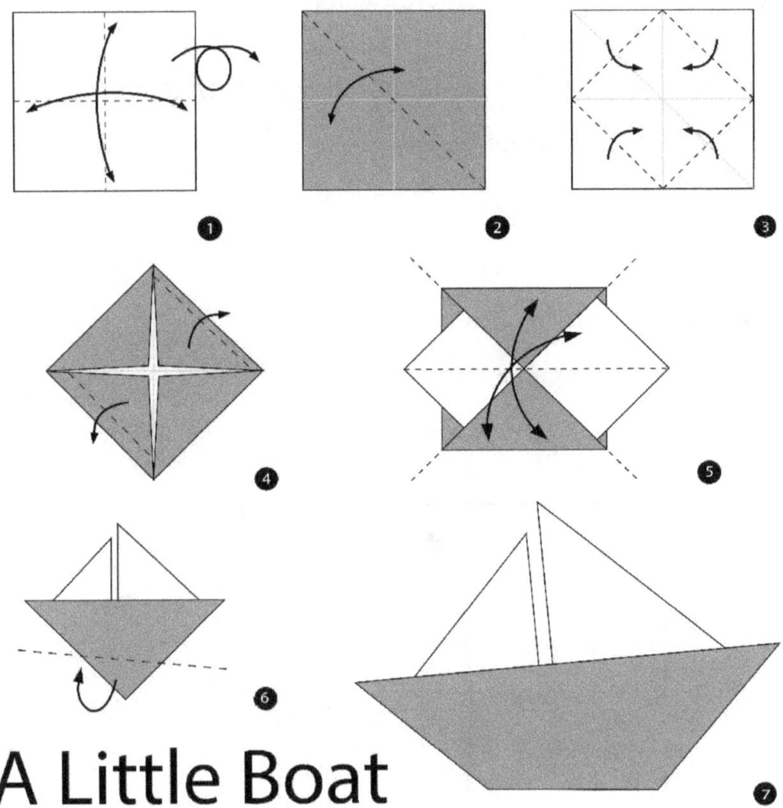

Japan is an island. It is surrounded by water on all sides. In the years before airplanes were invented, the Japanese had to travel by boat if they wanted to visit China, Korea, or even the United States.

The Japanese have a long history of making boats, which is why boats are very popular origami figures.

Although a big boat made out of paper probably wouldn't make it across the ocean, an *origami* boat made out of paper just might make it across a bathtub or sink filled with water!

This pattern is not too difficult, but it still offers the opportunity to learn some new folds. Here we go....

Step 1

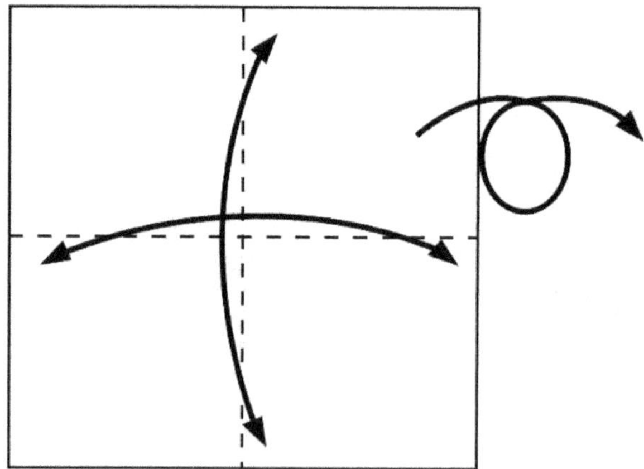

You'll notice that this time there are no corners facing you (or facing away from you). Place the square flat as shown, then fold it in half left to right and up and down.

Remember the looping arrow symbol? That means you need to turn the square over and make the same two folds on the other side of the paper.

Step 2

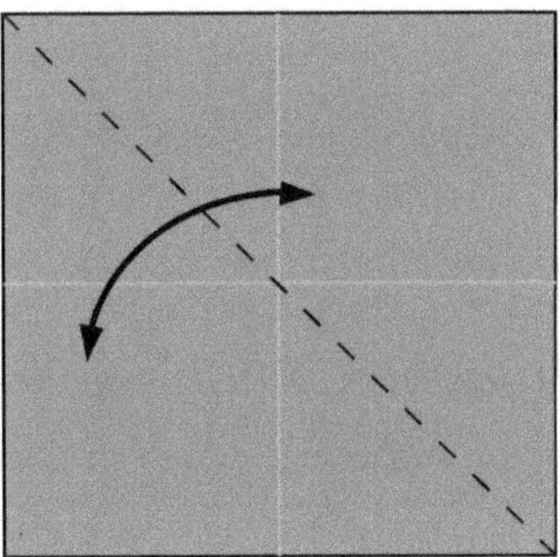

With the paper now face-down on the table, fold it in half diagonally as shown in the picture, then unfold it.

Step 3

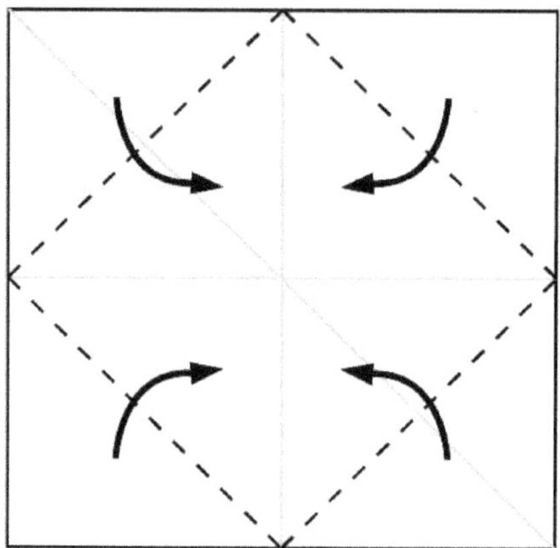

This step has four folds, so look at the picture carefully.

Don't panic, it's a lot simpler than it looks.

Notice the solid gray lines. At this point, you should have three creases in your paper: up and down, side to side, and diagonally.

The first thing you're going to do is turn the paper over again and return it to its original position.

The next thing you're going to do is take each corner and fold it as shown, so that each corner touches the very center of the square.

That's a lot of folding for one step, so if this is confusing to you in any way, don't hesitate to look ahead at the picture in **Step 4**; it should make everything clear.

Step 4

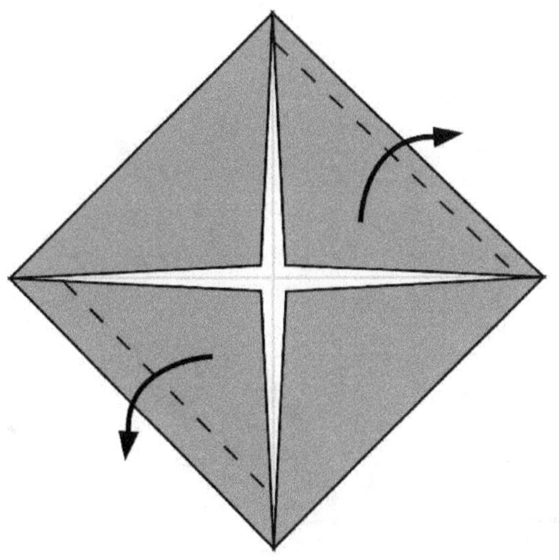

Take a good look at the dotted lines in the picture. You'll notice that they're a little different from each other. The one at the top is closer to the side than the one at the bottom. This will be important later, so make sure you notice it now and make your folds correctly.

Let's start with the top right corner. Take the corner and fold it back from the center in the direction of the arrow. Make sure that the fold is close to its side, as shown in the picture.

Now let's move to the bottom left corner. Take that corner and fold it back from the center in the direction of the arrow. Make sure that this fold is a little farther away from its side, as shown in the picture. This will be important in just a moment.

Step 5

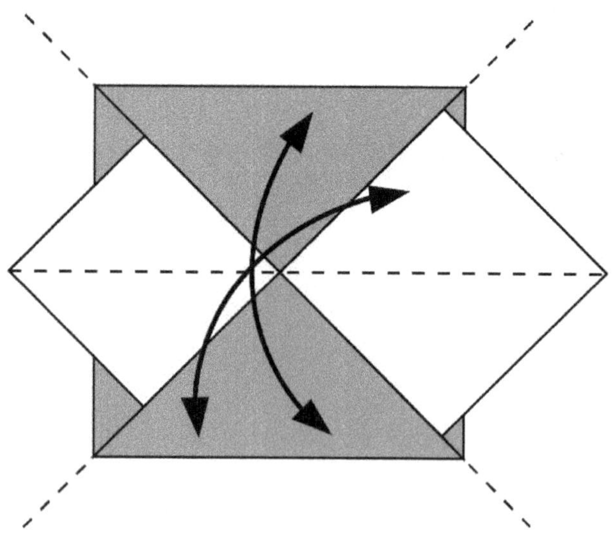

This step will fold the square in half three ways.

The first fold will be up and down, as shown by the dotted lines. The second fold and third folds, also shown by the dotted lines, will be diagonal. Take the bottom left corner and fold it up to the top right corner. For the third fold, again follow the dotted lines and fold the bottom right corner up to the top left corner.

Step 6

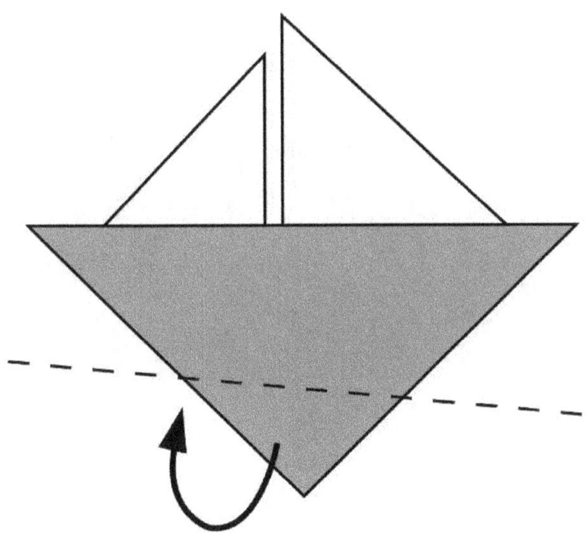

You now only have one more fold.

Take the bottom point (which is facing you) and fold it back behind the boat. Make sure you make the fold at a slight angle as shown in the picture. Although you don't *have* to do it at an angle, it makes the boat look cuter and somehow more realistic.

Ahoy! You Did It!

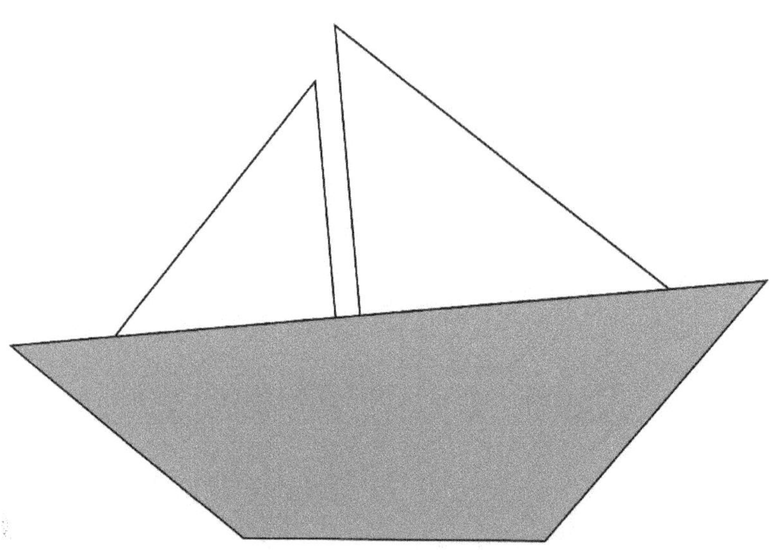

This little boat can sit proudly on your desk, or, if you're adventurous, it can float in your tub or sink.

Good job!

Chapter Ten: A Headfish

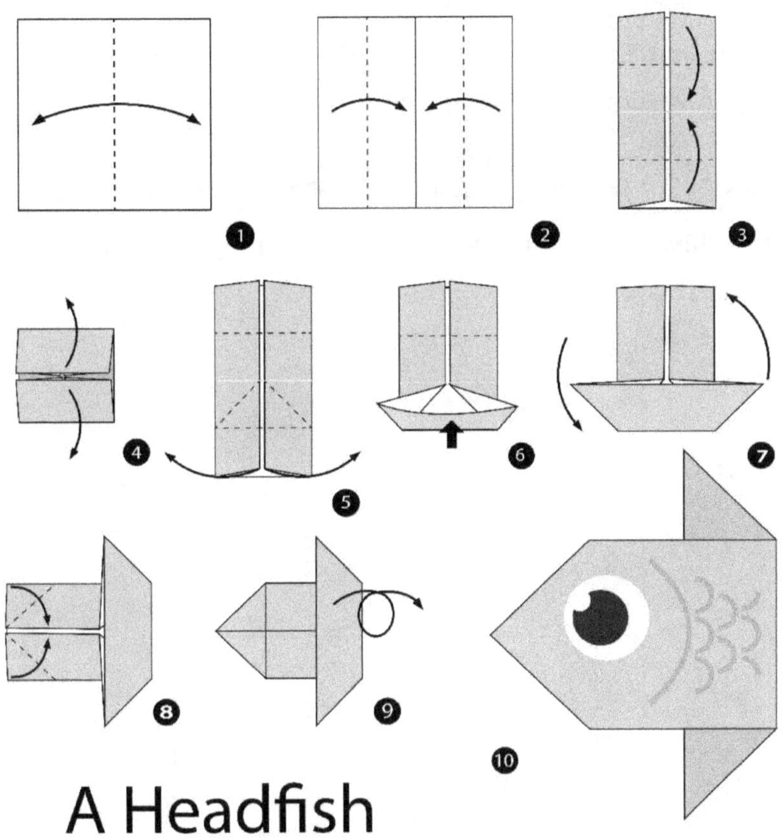

A Headfish

Well, now that you have a boat, it's time to go fishing!

The seas that surround Japan are full of fish, and the Japanese have a great love of fishing and of eating seafood. A headfish is an unusual creature that gets its name from its weird shape: it's body appears to be mostly head. They're actually a type of sunfish and are considered in Japan a real treat.

Luckily for us, the headfish's odd shape makes it an easy origami to learn. Plus, it will allow you to use your magic markers and plastic googly eyes.

Step 1

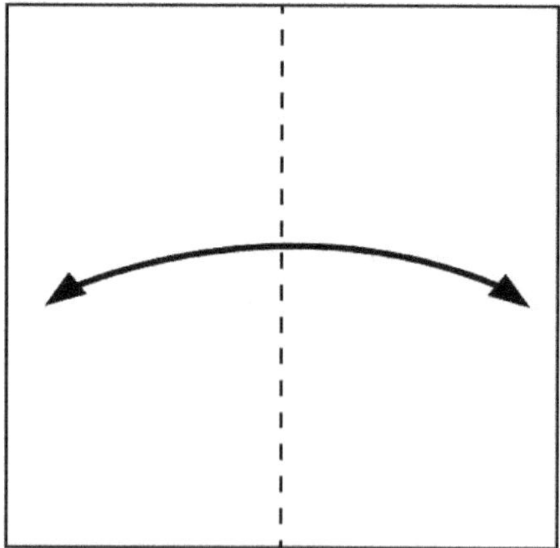

Place the paper flat on the table as in the picture. Fold it in half.

Step 2

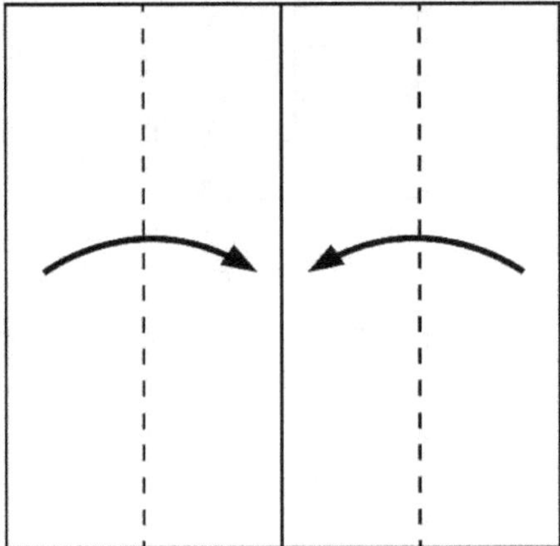

Unfold the paper and smooth it flat in the table again. You're now going to make two new folds, one from the right side and one from the left side. Basically, you're going to fold each half *in half*. Got that? Just remember to fold each side toward the center crease.

Step 3

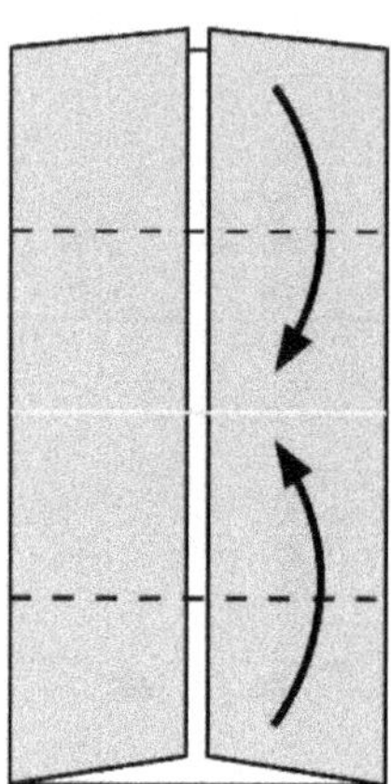

You're again going to make two folds in this step. Starting at the bottom, fold the bottom half of the paper upward, until the bottom side reaches the middle. Do you see that solid white line across the middle of the picture? That's the imaginary middle of the paper. Bring the bottom side of your paper upward and make it even with that.

Now do the same thing, only this time from the top.

Step 4

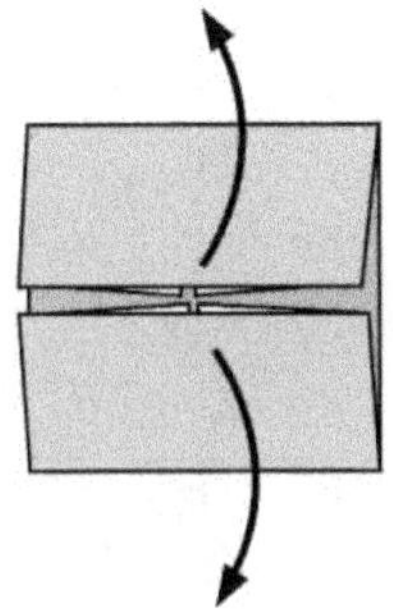

This step is very simple: just unfold the top and bottom so that the paper looks just like it did at the start of **Step 3**.

Step 5

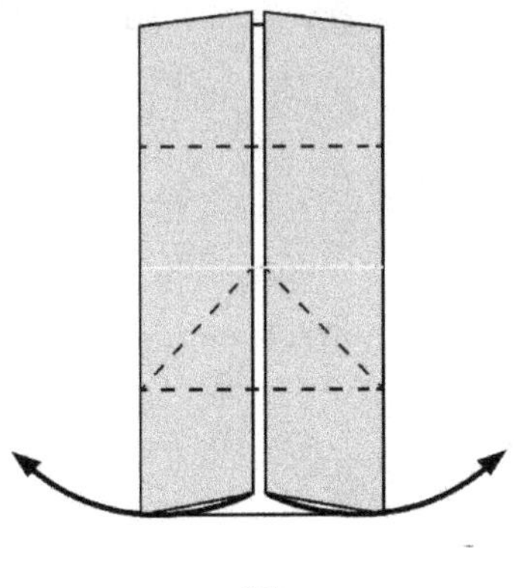

Make folds along the diagonal dotted lines, as you see in the picture.

Step 6

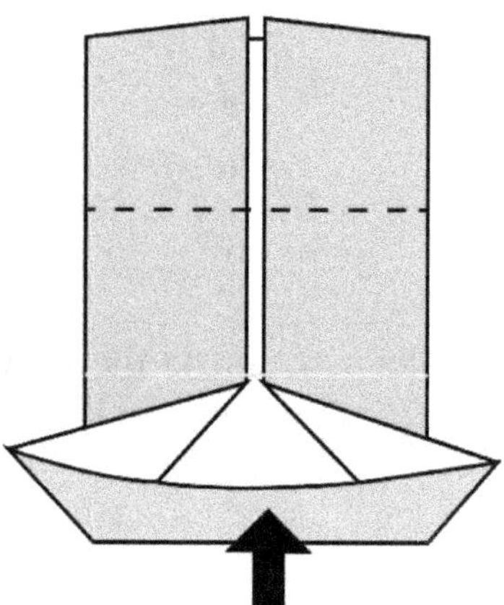

This next move looks a little hard, but once you start doing it, you'll see that it's actually very easy. Just pull the very bottom side down and out, then fold it back up, pressing against the diagonal creases you just made in **Step 5**.

Step 7

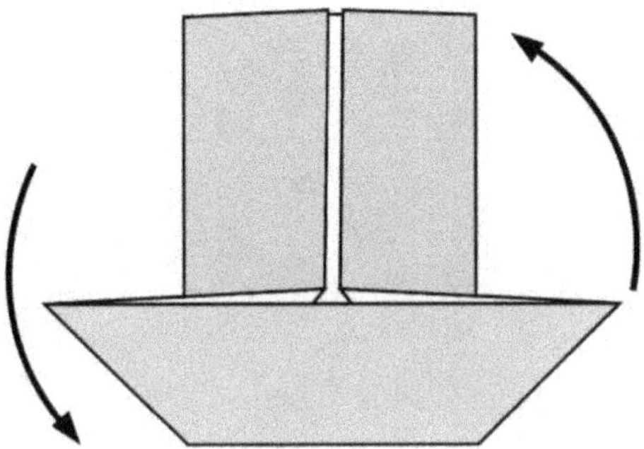

This is what your paper should look like now. The next thing to do is turn it sideways to the left.

Step 8

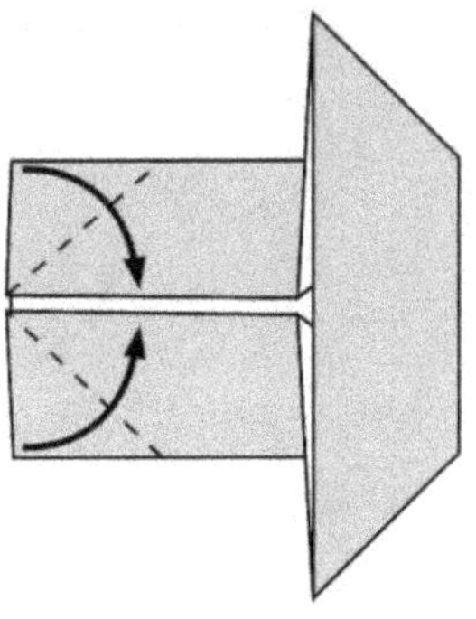

Now make fold along the dotted diagonal lines, like you see in the picture. Just be sure to fold the paper *toward* you.

Step 9

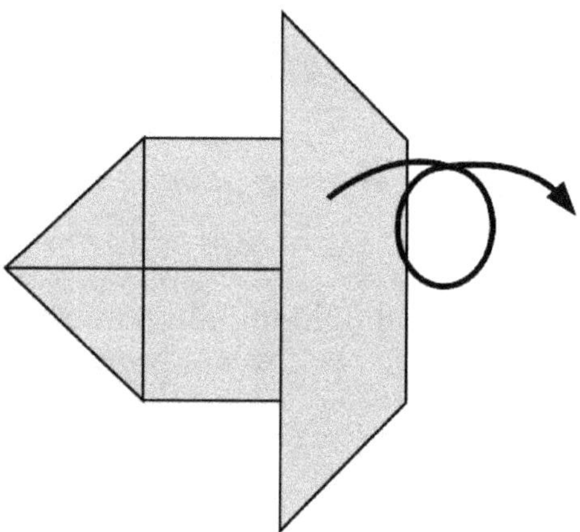

This is what your paper should look like now. Do you see the looping arrow? That means to turn the paper over.

Step 10

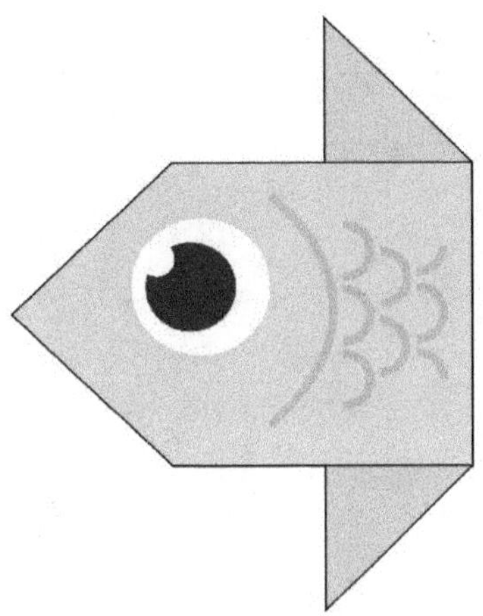

Almost there…

Grab a magic marker and draw some scales and a gill. Then take one of the plastic googly eyes you got at the craft store and stick it on your headfish.

You're done!

Chapter Eleven: A Peacock

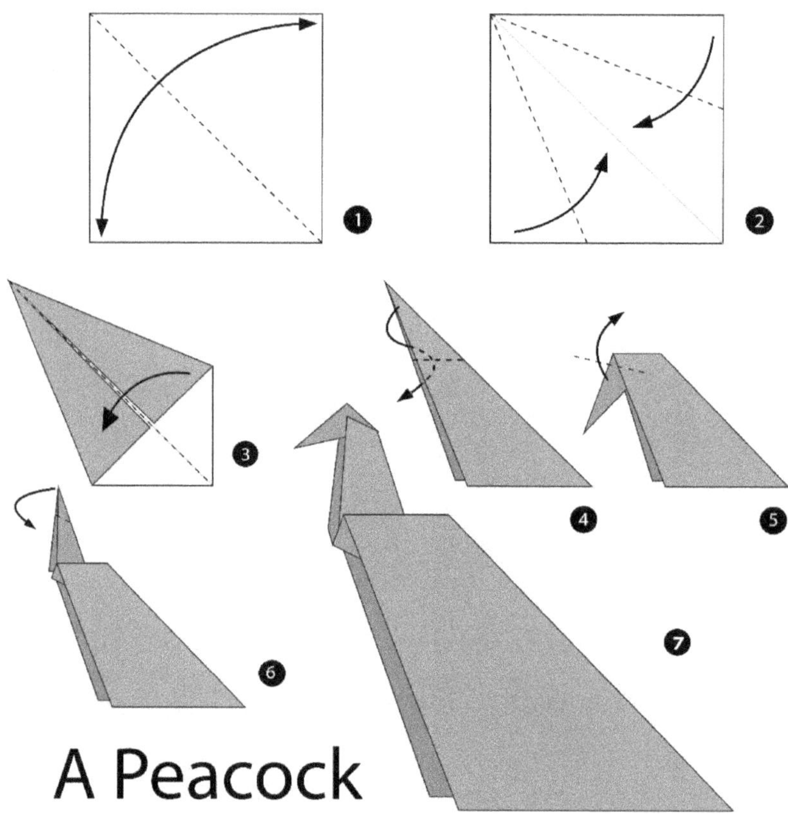

Back in Chapter Six you made a bird. What kind of bird was it? Whatever kind of bird you wanted it to be.

This time, though, you're going to make a specific kind of bird. This time, you're going to make a peacock.

The peacock is a symbol of compassion and kind-heartedness, and it is believed to have the power to defeat poison and even make it rain. In Japanese culture, it is associated with good health. The peacock is a good symbol and a good origami to make.

Step 1

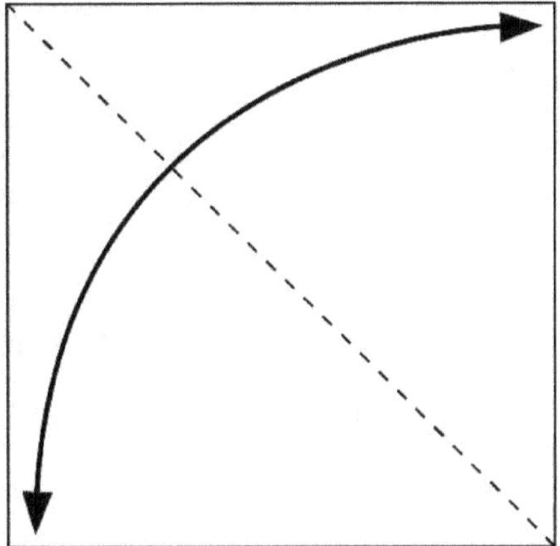

Place the square flat on the table as shown and fold it in half diagonally. Bring the bottom left corner up to the top right corner, make a crease, then unfold the paper.

Step 2

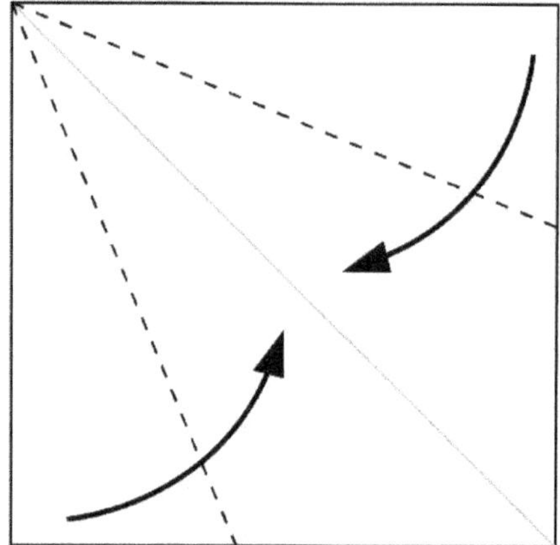

This next fold will be familiar to anyone who's ever made a paper airplane. Fold the top right corner down along the dotted line, so that the top of the square is even with the center crease.

Now do the same thing with the bottom left corner.

Step 3

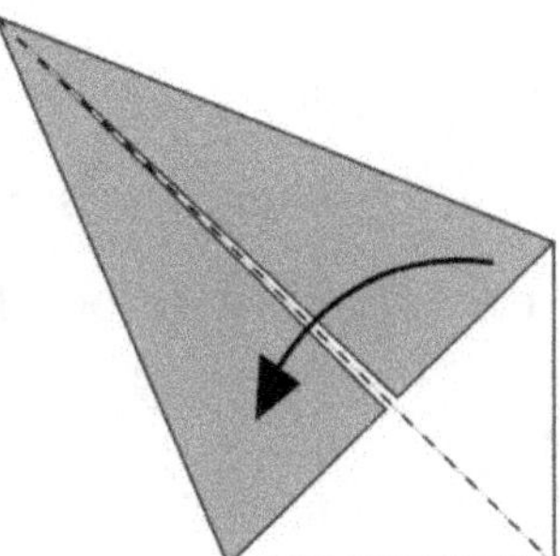

Now fold the figure in half, as shown. It kind of looks like you're about to make a paper airplane, but you're not.

Step 4

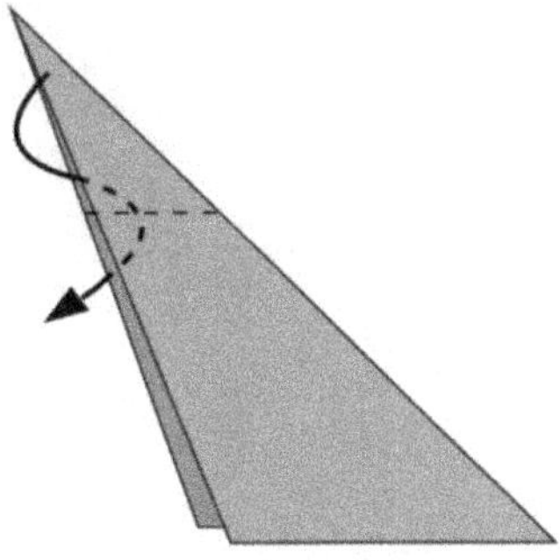

This next move is kind of neat.

Fold the paper near the top, as shown by the dotted lines. Fold the paper both ways.

Then, here comes the neat part: you're going to take that top point and follow the arrow down. In other words, you're going to "turn the paper inside out," so that the figure will look like the picture in **Step 5** below.

Step 5

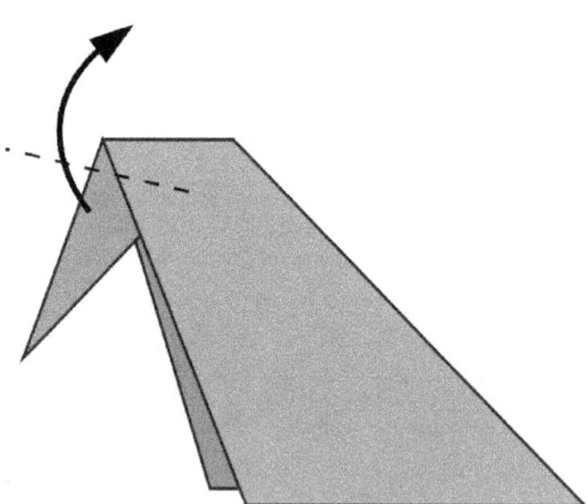

Now reverse what you just did and bring the point back up—but make a fold along the dotted lines as you do it.

Step 6

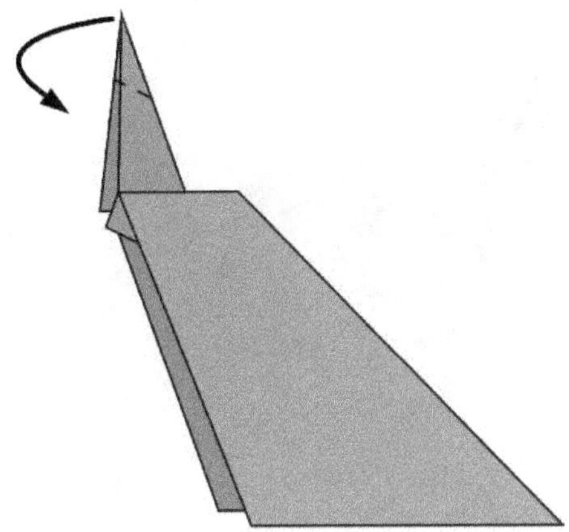

The only thing left for you to do now is make the beak. You do this by making a fold along the dotted lines, then by pushing the paper inside the figure and flattening it along the creases you've already made. By the way, this type of origami fold is called an inside reverse fold.

Success!

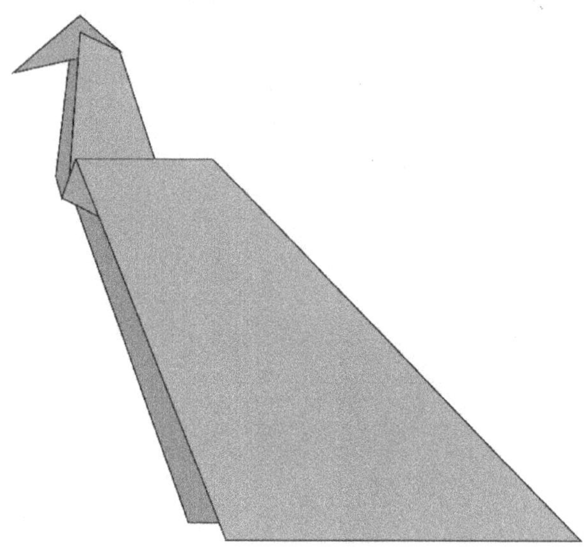

You've completed your second bird, this one a majestic peacock. You're on a roll!

Chapter Twelve: A Fox Face

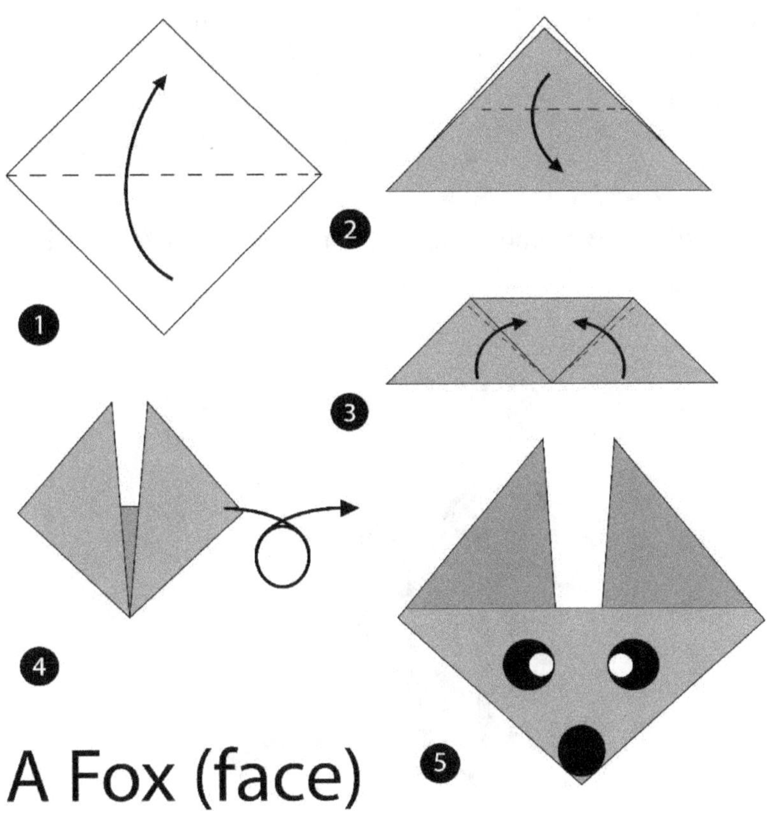

A Fox (face)

What do you say we take a little break and relax?

That last pattern was a kind of complex, so maybe you'd like to catch your breath and enjoy an easy one.

Plus, this pattern will give you an excuse to use some more googly eyes.

But first, did you know that the Japanese word for fox is *kitsune*? Here it is:

In ancient Japan, foxes and humans lived closely together, and this closeness generated legends about the creatures. Foxes were seen as somehow supernatural and were believed to be the messengers of spirits and gods. In many Japanese folktales, foxes have the ability to change into humans—sometimes to trick humans, sometimes to help them.

Now that you know a little about the *kitsune*, or fox, it's time to make one!

Step 1

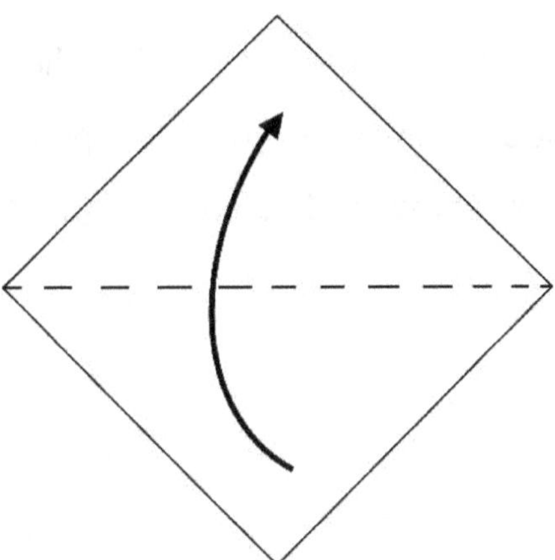

Position the paper so that one of the squares is facing away from you. Fold it in half along the dotted line.

Step 2

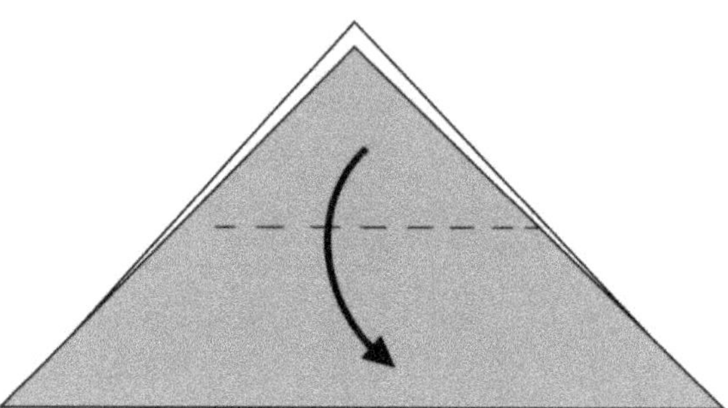

Take the two corners pointing up and fold them (both of them, not just one of them) down towards you. The points should touch the bottom of the paper, as shown in **Step 3**.

Step 3

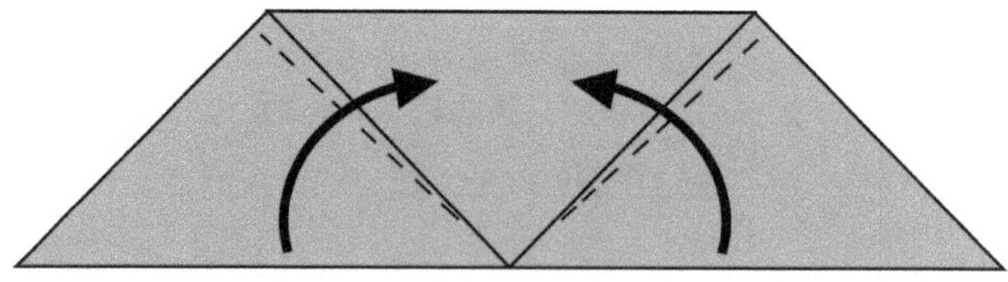

Now you're going to make some fox ears.

Take each of the corners and fold them up, following the arrows.

Step 4

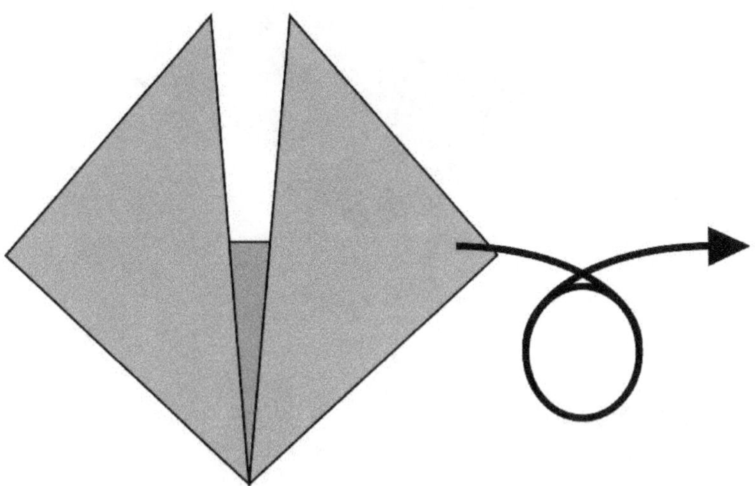

Are you starting to see it?

You know what that looping arrow means.

Turn the whole thing over.

Step 5

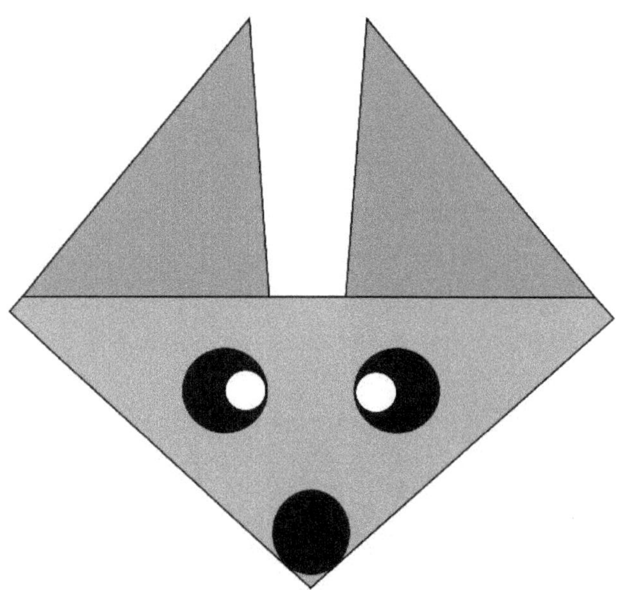

It's googly eye time!

Take your magic marker and fill in a round little nose for your fox. Then stick some googly eyes on it and you're done!

Chapter Thirteen: A Cat

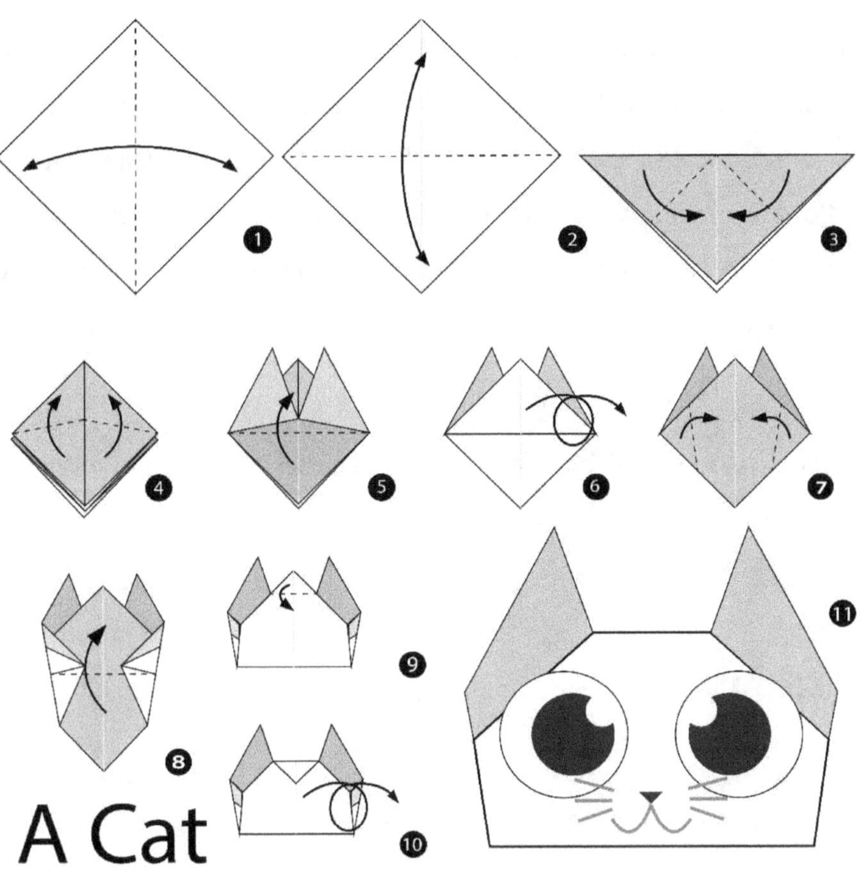

Have you ever seen someone with a headfish for a pet? Me neither. But you probably *have* seen lots of people with *cats* for pets. Cats are among the most popular animals on the planet, so it's fitting that they should be popular among origami artists.

In Japan, cats are believed to bring good luck and other positive results. There is a popular Japanese cat figurine called "beckoning cat" that is often given as a gift to bring blessings. The figurine usually has a cat with its paw raised, as if waving hello or calling you over. According to Japanese legend, a landlord witnessed a cat waving a paw at him. Intrigued, he came close to the cat. Suddenly a lightning bolt struck the exact spot where he had been previously standing. The landlord believed that his good fortune was because of the cat's actions. Ever since then, the beckoning cat has been a symbol of good luck. These little figurines are mostly found at the entrances of shops, restaurants, and other businesses.

This pattern will be a little challenging, so pay close attention to the pictures.

Step 1

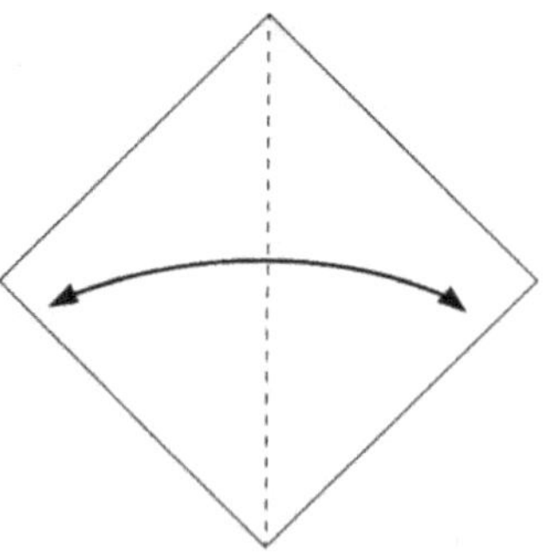

As you so often do, you'll start with the paper flat on the table with a corner facing away from you. Fold the paper in half down the middle, from side to side.

Step 2

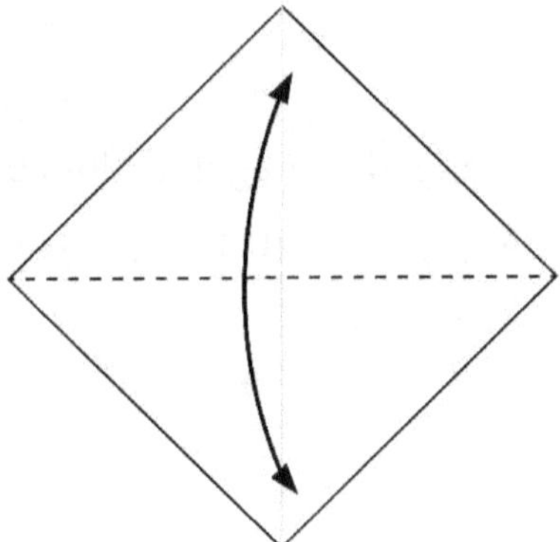

Now fold the square again, this time up and down. Bring the top corner and place it on top of the bottom corner, so that you have a triangle with a point facing towards you.

Step 3

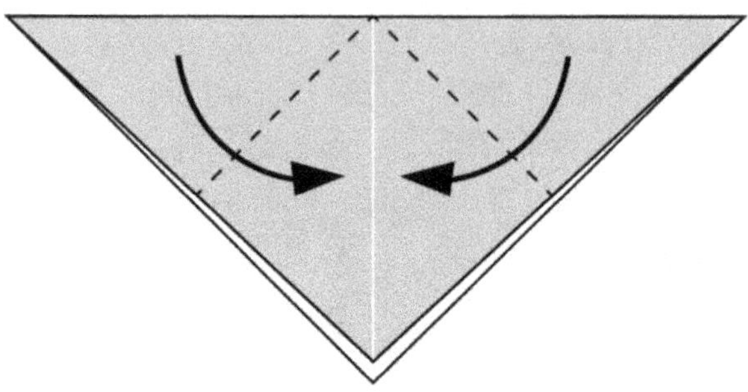

Now make folds along the diagonal dotted lines in the picture. Always remember to bend your folds in the direction of the arrows.

Step 4

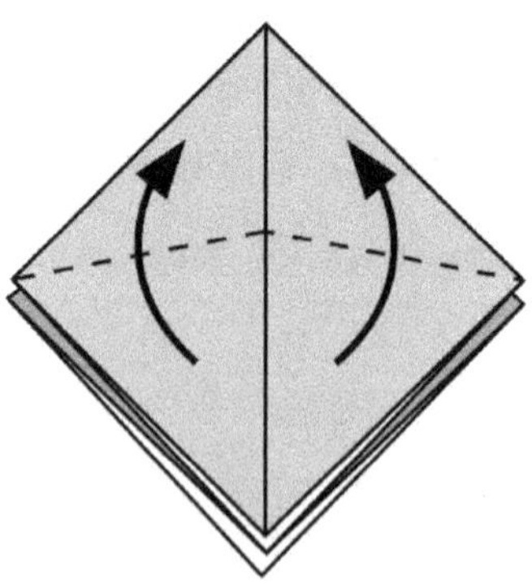

You should have two small flaps pointing toward you now. They're on top. Pull the two flaps up and fold them along the dotted lines so that they're pointing away from you.

Step 5

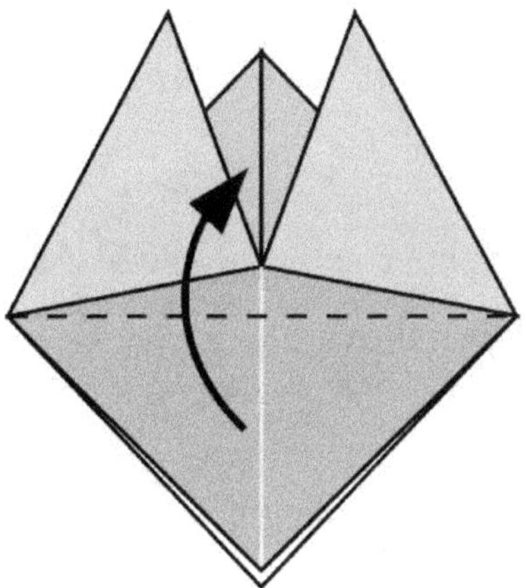

When you fold those two smaller flaps up, you reveal a larger flap that's pointing toward you. Fold *that* flap up and crease it along the dotted line.

Step 6

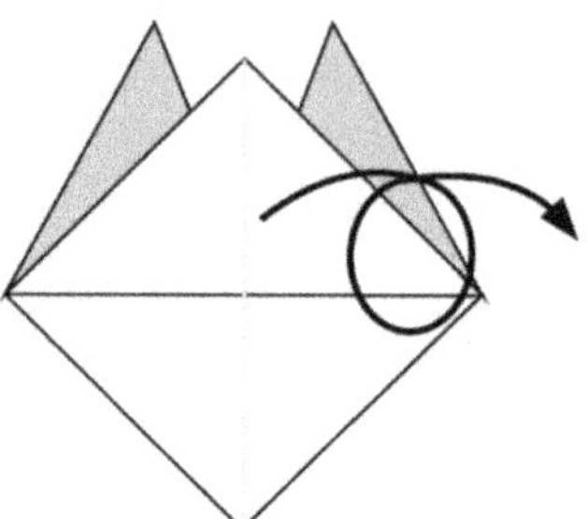

This is what your paper should look like at this point. Now take the whole pattern and turn it over.

Step 7

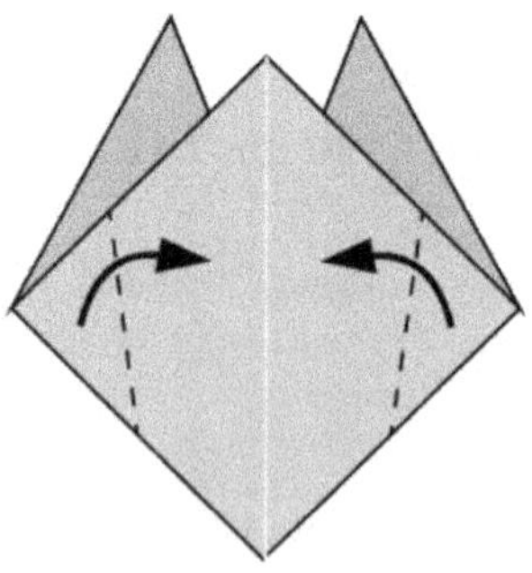

Take each side and fold the points inward, toward the center crease (the solid gray line you see in the picture). But make sure the points don't actually *touch* the center crease. Look at the drawing in **Step 8** if you're unsure how far to fold your points.

Step 8

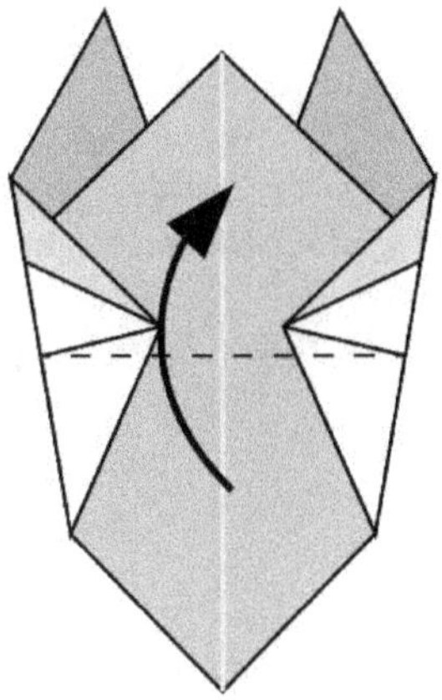

Now you're going to fold the entire pattern in half. Take the bottom point (which is pointing toward you) and fold it up so that it is even with the top point (which is facing away from you).

Step 9

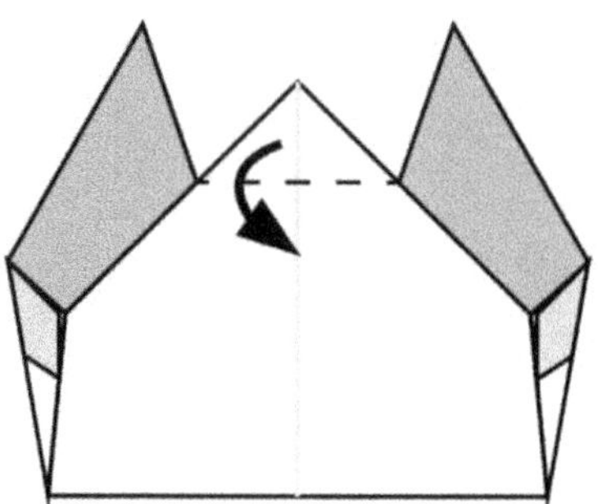

Take the back point and fold it down (towards you) along the
dotted line you see in the drawing.

Step 10

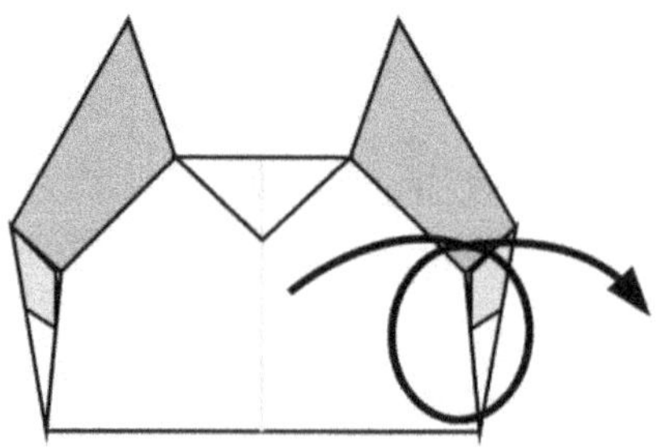

Now flip the entire pattern over.

Step 11

Take a black or brown magic marker and draw some whiskers on your cat face. Remember that cat's noses are shaped like upside-down triangles. When you take your marker and draw a nose for your cat, make it look like the one in the picture above.

Then take two plastic googly eyes and stick them on the paper.

Congratulations! You've made yourself a cute origami cat!

Chapter Fourteen: A Tulip

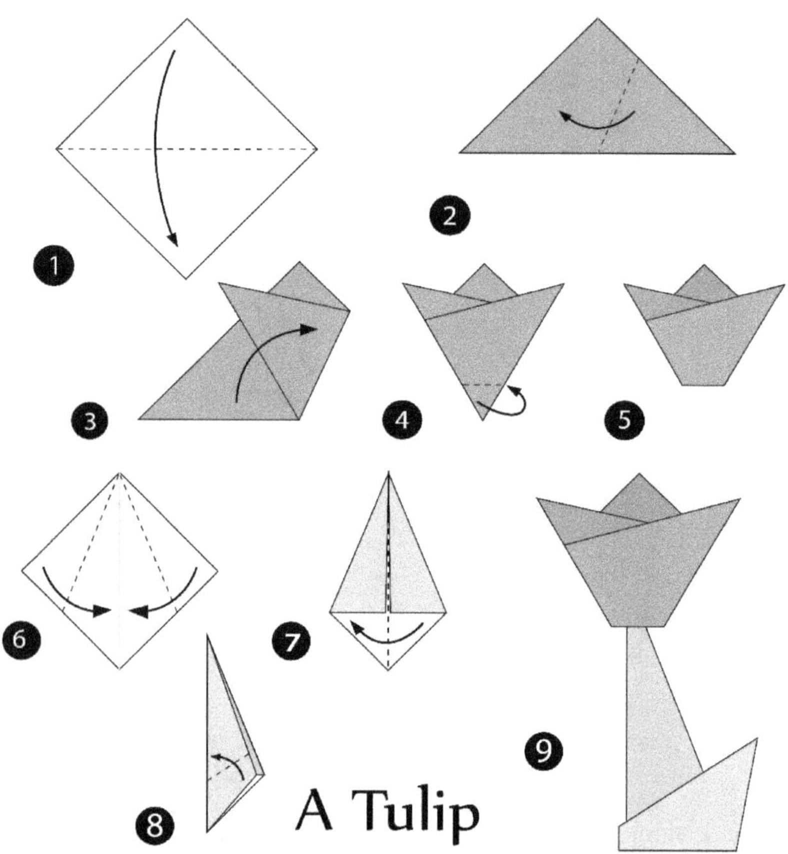

In Japan, tulips bloom in late April and early May, and make the springtime bright and colorful. They are very popular flowers in Japan. In fact, in Tokyo (which, if you'll remember from Chapter One, used to be called Edo), there is a big tulip festival every year that attracts thousands of people.

This is a simple pattern, but it requires something new: a second piece of paper.

Step 1

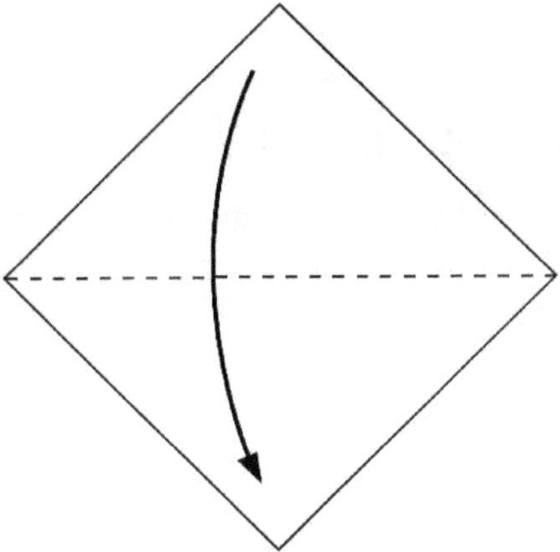

Place the paper so that one of the corners is facing away from you. Fold the paper in half, bringing the bottom to the top.

Step 2

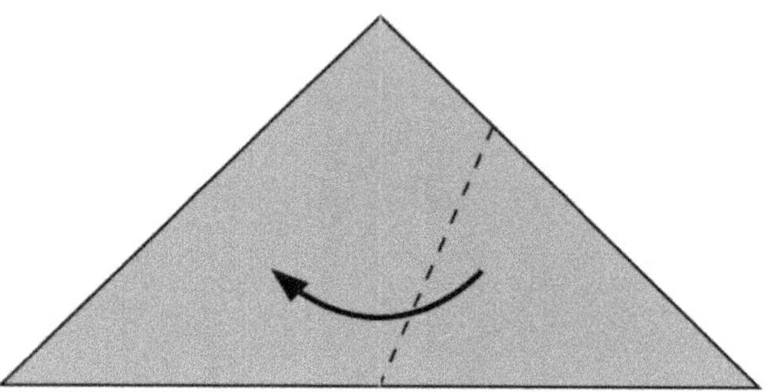

Make a fold along the dotted line shown in the drawing above. This is similar to the fold you made earlier with the cup.

Step 3

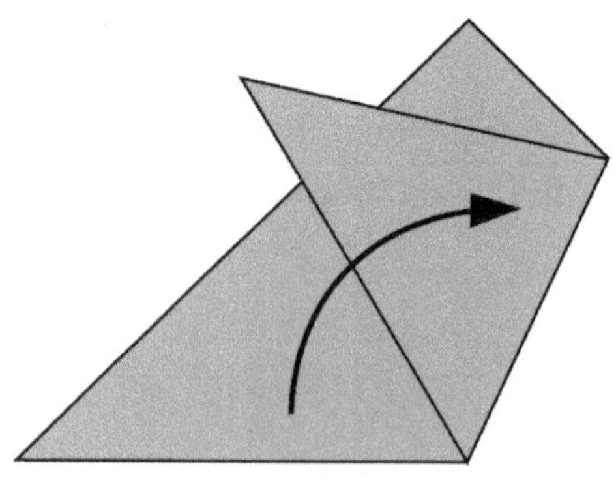

Once you have folded the right corner over, do the same thing with the left corner, folding in the direction of the arrow.

Step 4

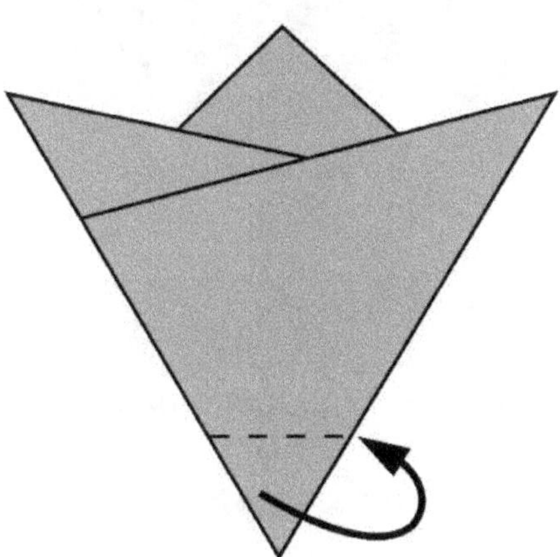

Take the point that's facing you and fold it behind the flower.

Step 5

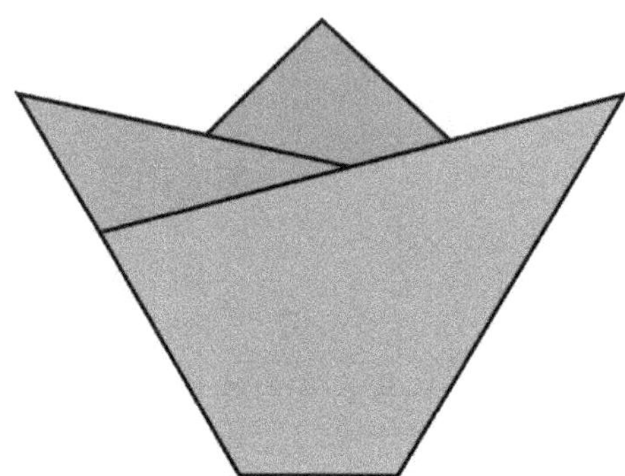

Your flower is finished! Well, not quite. It doesn't have a stem!

Step 6

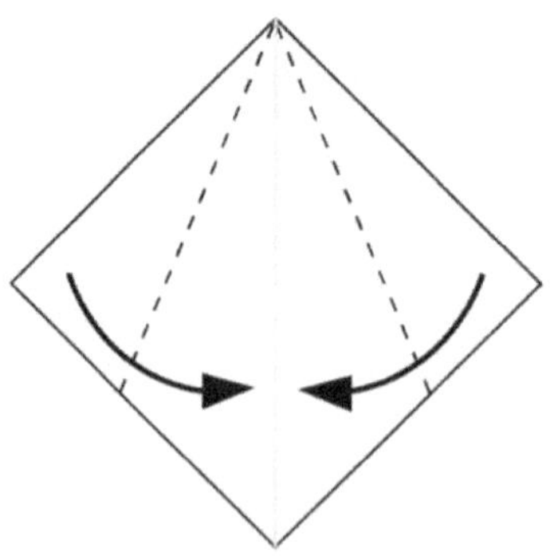

Get a second square of paper and place it on the table with a corner facing away from you. Fold it in half straight down the middle, top to bottom. Unfold it. Then make two more folds along the dotted lines. You made this fold before when learning the peacock.

Step 7

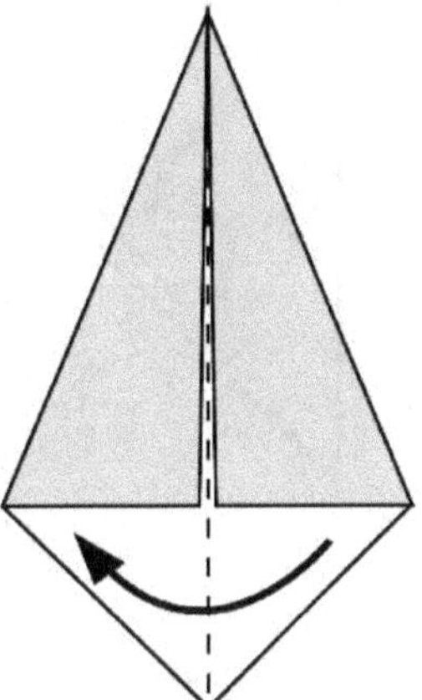

Fold the paper down the middle again, bringing the right corner over to the left corner.

Step 8

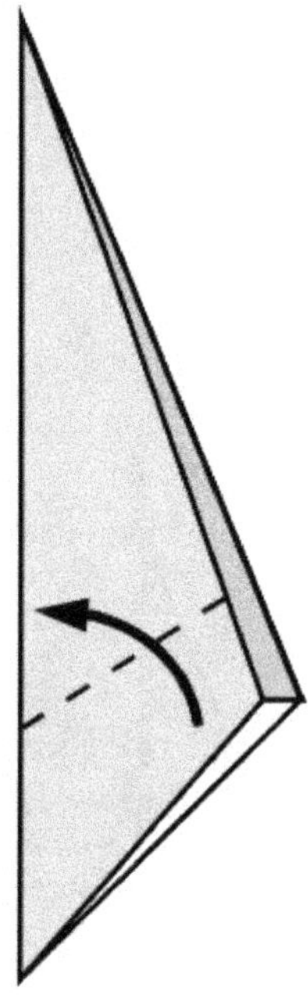

Make a fold along the dotted line shown and bend the paper in the direction of the arrow.

Step 9

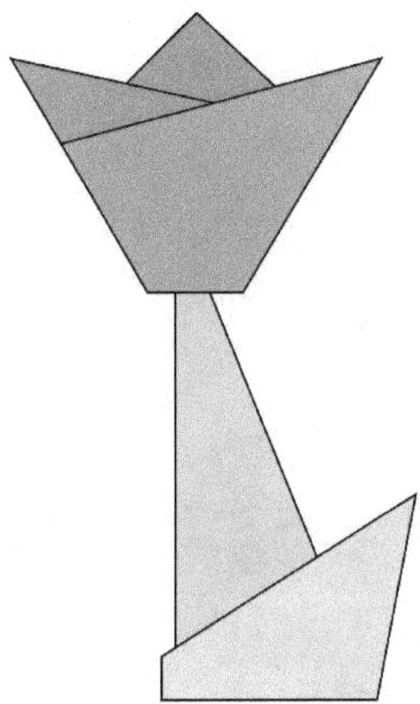

You're almost there.

All you have to do now is insert the top of the stem into the bottom of the tulip flower.

You're done!

Chapter Fifteen: A Whale

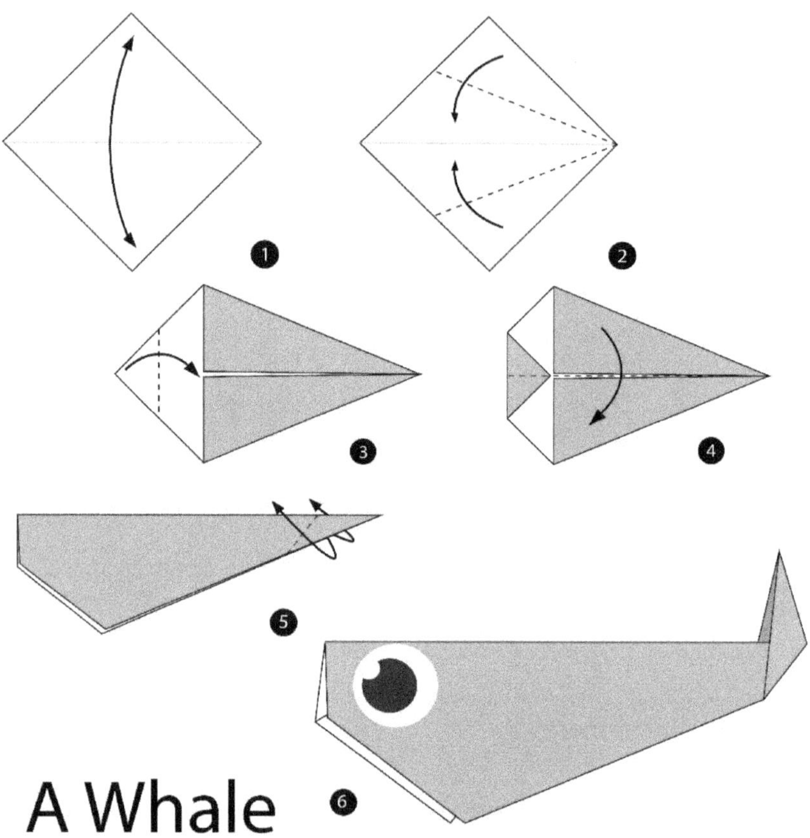

A Whale

As an island, Japan has a long history of living off the bounty of the sea. There are a lot of whales in the waters around Japan, and the Japanese people have always felt a closeness to them (and often used them for food). Here's a cute and easy design of that giant of the ocean—the whale.

Step 1

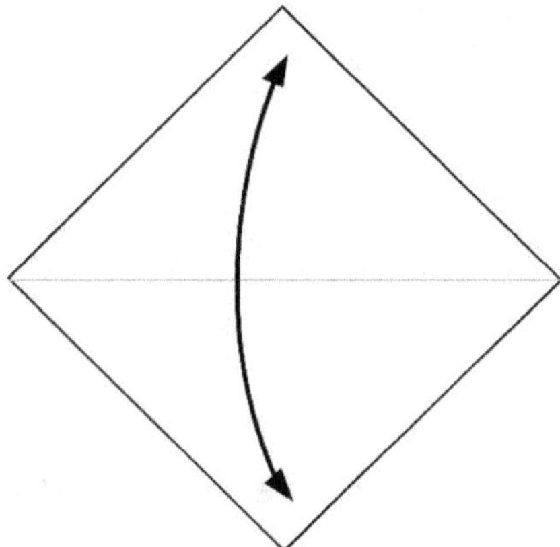

Place the paper flat on the table, and make sure that one of the corners is facing away from you. Fold the paper in half as shown in the picture. Then unfold it.

Step 2

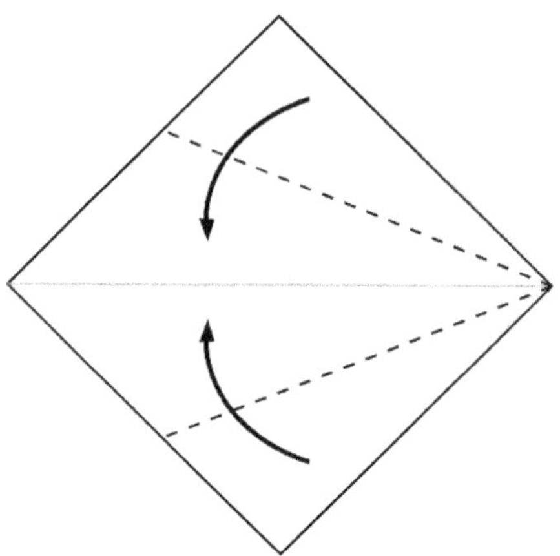

These are folds that you've made before and should be comfortable with by now. Take the top corner (the one facing away from you) and fold it so that its top right side is even with the crease from **Step 1** (that crease is represented by the solid gray line). Now do the same thing from the bottom. Take the bottom corner (the one facing you) and fold it up so that its left side is even with the crease from **Step 1**.

Step 3

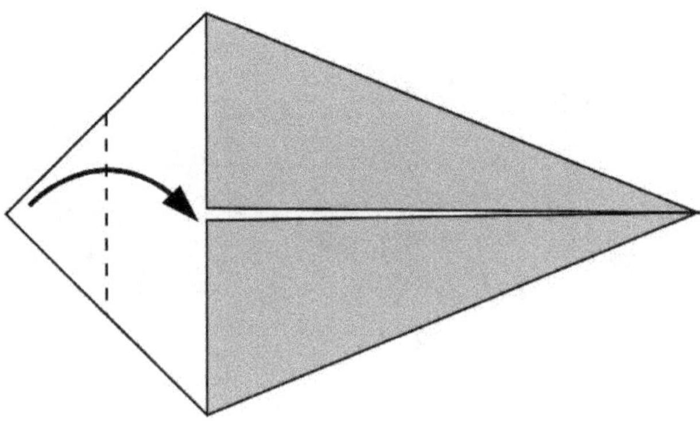

Rotate the paper so that the longest point is facing to the right, as shown in the picture above. At this stage, the shape of your paper somewhat resembles an arrowhead.

Take the point that's facing left and fold it along the dotted line you see in the picture. The point that was facing left should now almost be touching the two flaps.

Step 4

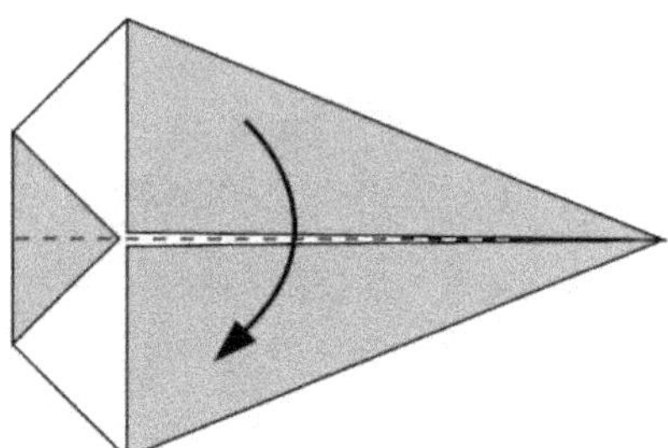

This kind of looks like you're building a paper airplane again, doesn't it?

Fold the paper in half as shown in the drawing. Bring the top half and fold it over the bottom half.

Step 5

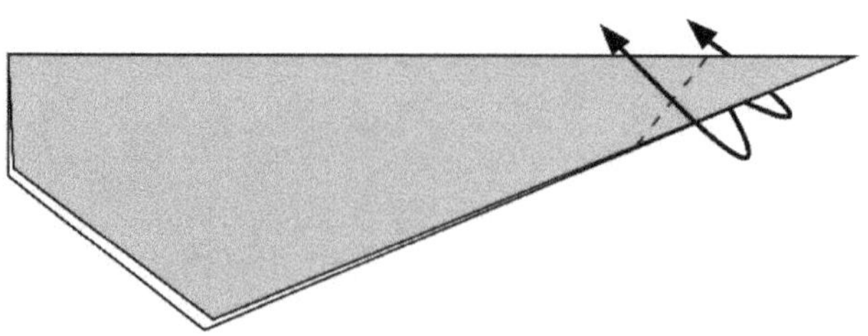

Now you're going to make what's called an outside reverse fold.

Do you see the dotted line in the drawing? Fold the paper along that line. First fold it to the left, then fold it to the right. Make sure you have a good crease.

Now partially unfold the paper and flip the flap over, following the direction of the arrows in the drawing.

Step 6

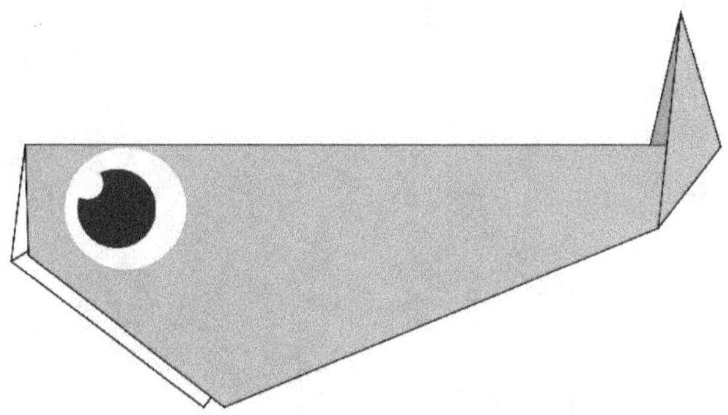

By making an outside reverse fold, you have given your whale a tail! The only thing left to do is give him—or her—an eye. You can draw one with a dark magic marker, or you can glue on a plastic googly eye. And you're done!

Chapter Sixteen: A Brachiosaur

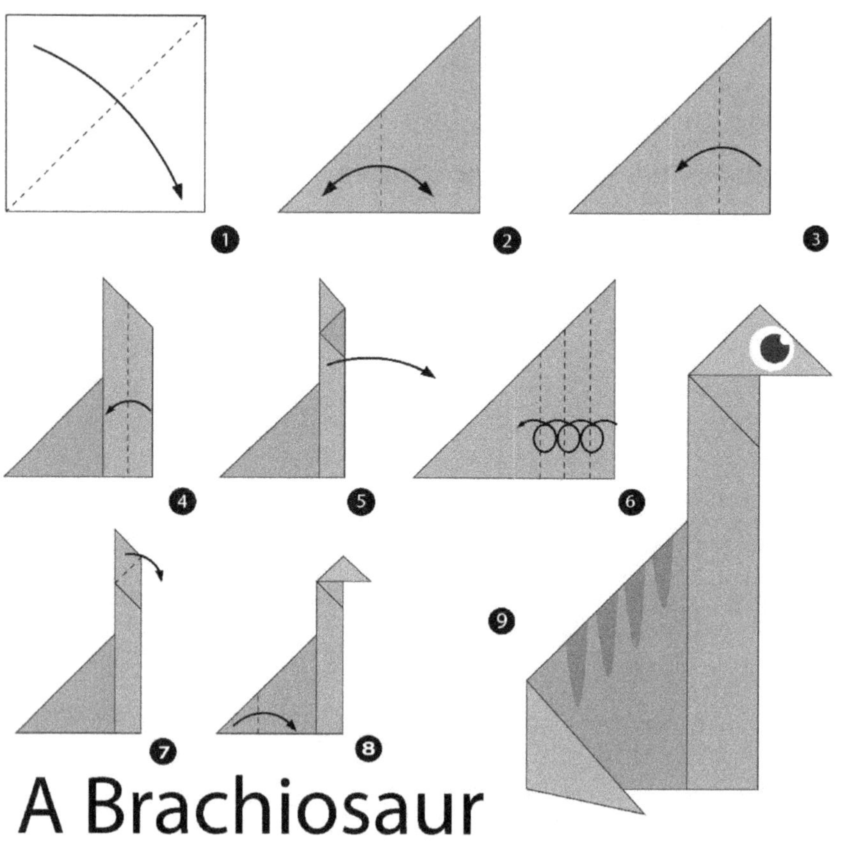

Unlike the other animals you've made so far, the brachiosaur no longer exists. They disappeared from earth millions and millions of years ago, though scientists aren't exactly sure why. Brachiosaurs were *huge*: they were around 80 feet long and weighed more than 60 tons! But unlike the aggressive tyrannosaurs, the brachiosaurs were very gentle and ate grass and vegetables. They were actually kind of cute for a dinosaur, which is why we're going to make one now.

Step 1

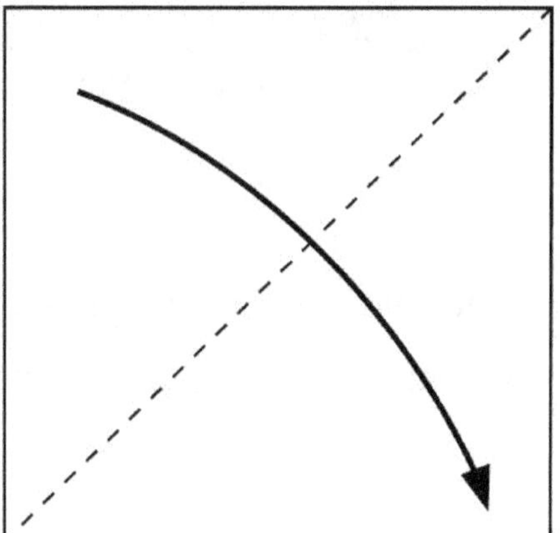

Lay the paper flat on the table. None of the corners should be facing towards you or away from you. Fold the paper in half as shown in the drawing. Take the top left corner and fold it, following the direction of the arrow, till it meets the bottom right corner.

Step 2

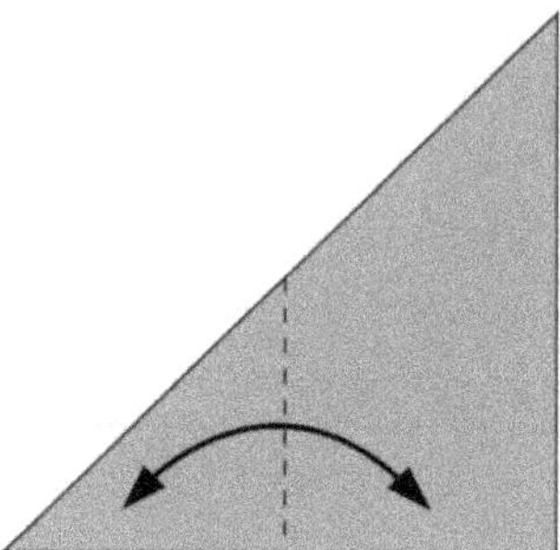

Now you're going to fold the new bottom left corner as shown in the picture. Fold it, then unfold it. Make sure there's a good crease.

Step 3

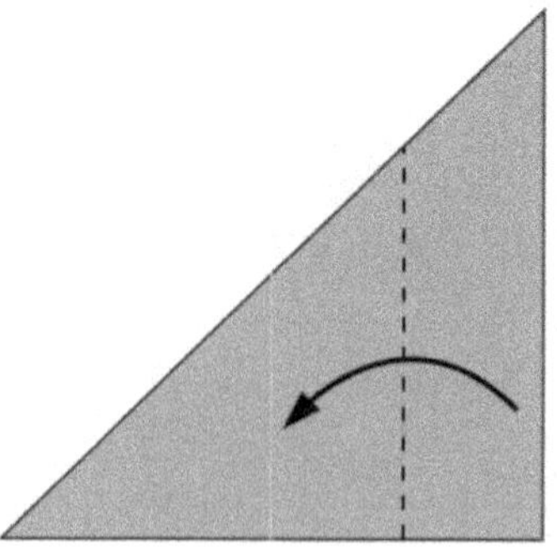

Make another fold, this time from the right. Fold the right side of the triangle so that its edge is even with the crease you made in **Step 2**.

Step 4

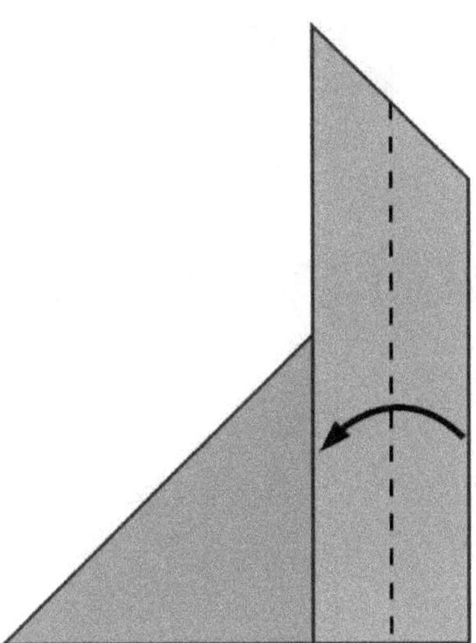

Take a look at the dotted line in the drawing. It sits halfway between the crease you made in **Step 2** and the new right side of your paper. Basically, you're going to fold the right side of your paper till it, too, is even with the crease you made in **Step 2**. You're doubling the fold.

Step 5

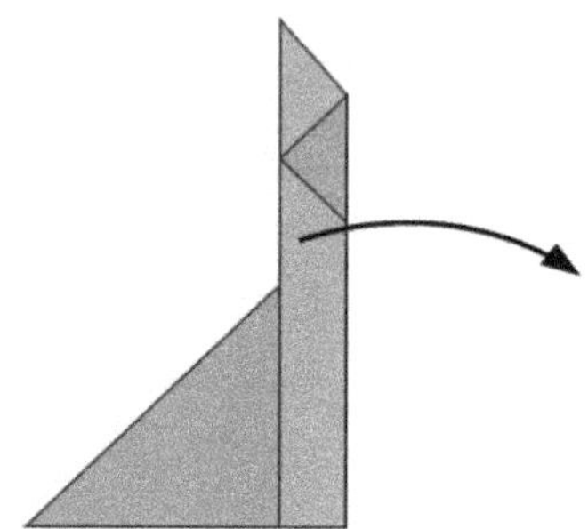

Unfold your paper and lay it out flat so you can see it.

Step 6

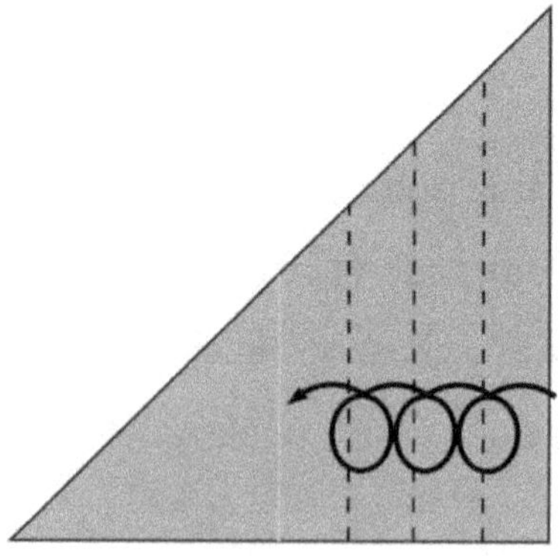

You can now see what you've done: you've made a series of folds across the paper. Make sure the crease of each fold is sharp.

Now refold the paper so that it resembles the figure you had at the beginning of **Step 5**.

Step 7

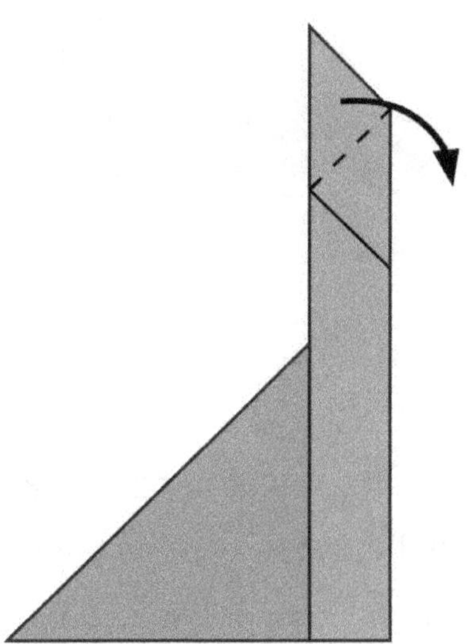

Fold the paper along the dotted line you see in the drawing. This will bring the point of the corner down so that it faces to the right. This will be the face of the brachiosaur.

Step 8

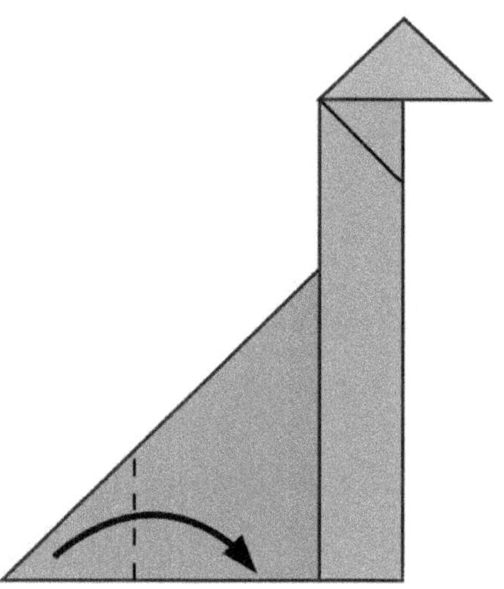

The only fold remaining will create the tail. Take the left corner and fold it to the right. Make sure the crease is good and crisp, because the brachiosaur's tail will need to sit at an angle. The angle will allow the brachiosaur origami to stay upright when you place it down on a table or other flat surface.

Step 9

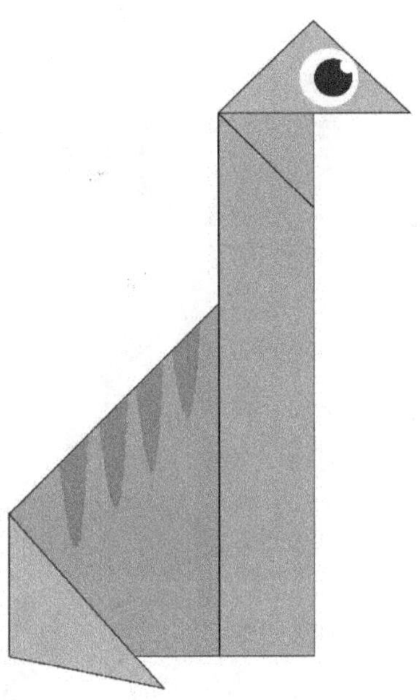

The only thing left to do is to give your brachiosaur a googly eye and, if you want, some patterns on its back. You can take one of your magic markers and follow the design in the picture, or you can come up with one of your own. It's entirely up to you!

And you're done! Well, except for naming your new pet…

Chapter Seventeen: A Crane

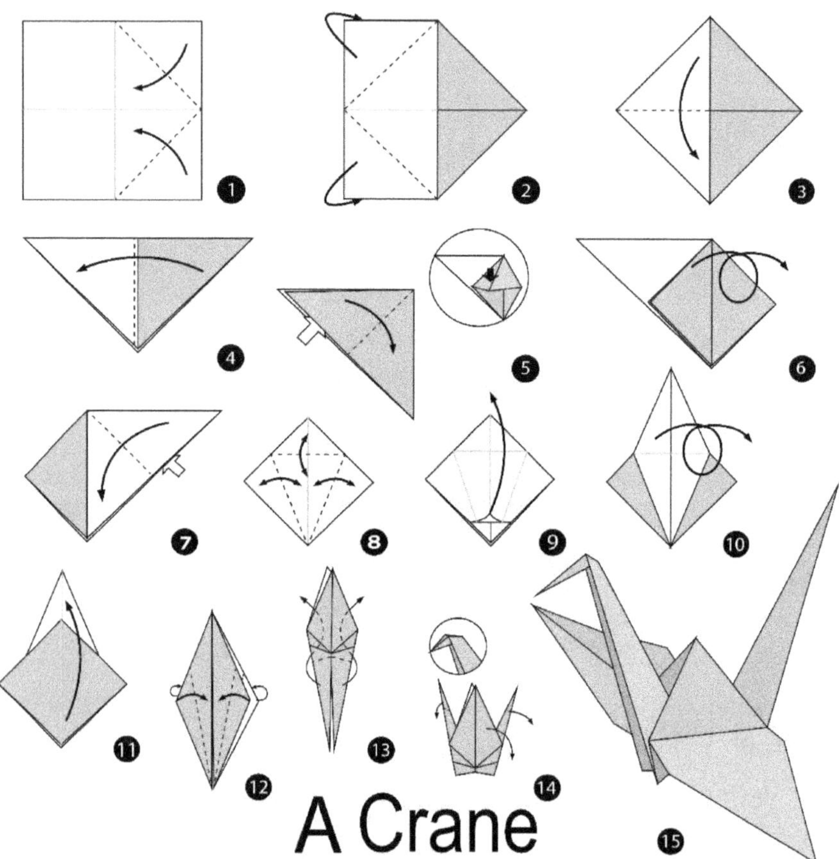

We come, at last, to the crane.

I've saved this origami figure for last because it's so very important in Japanese culture. In fact, it's so important that I want to take a minute and tell you about it before we start making one. This will be one of the most difficult patterns you will ever try. It is very complex…but also very beautiful. You will probably make a lot of mistakes and have to start over a few times. That's okay. Everybody does. Your hard work will be worth it, though.

The Crane in Japanese Culture

For the Japanese, cranes are elegant, mystical birds. For thousands of years, they've treasured the crane as a symbol of honor and loyalty. Hundreds of years ago, the Japanese believed that cranes lived for a thousand years. Because of this belief, the crane came to be seen as a sign of good luck and a long life in Japanese culture.

In Japan, the crane is known as "the bird of happiness." A long time ago, people believed that the wings of the crane carried souls to paradise. Even today, mothers who pray for the protection of their children will offer the following prayer:

O flock of heavenly cranes,

Cover my child with your wings…

Just over 200 years ago, one of the first books about origami was published in Japan. It was called *How to Fold 1,000 Cranes*. You're probably wondering: Why would anyone want to fold 1,000 origami cranes? That's a good question—and it has a surprising answer.

Traditionally, people in Japan believed that if someone folded 1,000 origami cranes, then anything that person wished for would come true. Because of this belief, cranes became not only a symbol of honor and loyalty, but also a symbol of hope and healing during tough times. As a result, a beautiful custom developed and remains to this day: people fold 1,000 paper cranes and string them together—usually there are 25 strings, and each string has 40 cranes. These are then given as gifts. The Japanese love the idea of 1,000 hand-folded cranes so much that they even have a name for it: *senbazuru*.

Cranes as a Symbol of Marriage

In Japan, cranes have become a symbol of marriage. Folding a crane takes time, patience, and understanding, just like marriage. Weddings in Japan are often decorated with 1,000 hand-folded cranes. Even more amazing is that the 1,000 cranes are hand-folded by the people getting married!

Now that you have some idea just how important cranes—and origami cranes, in particular--are, let's make one of our very own!

Step 1

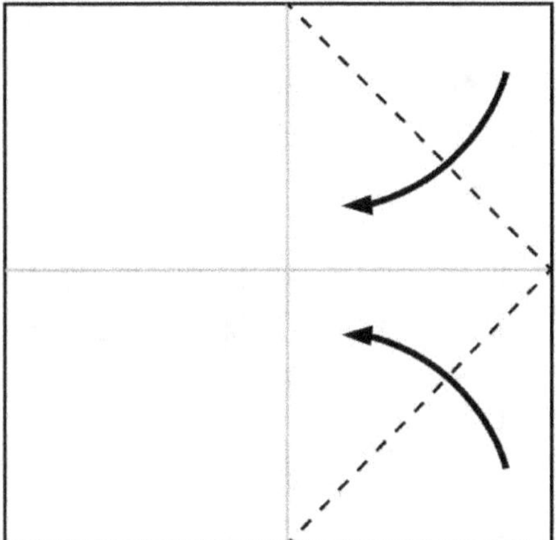

Here we go! Place the square flat on the table. There should be no corners pointing toward you. Fold the paper in half from side to side, then fold it up and down. Unfold your paper and smooth it flat on the table. You should have creases in your paper where the solid gray lines are in the drawing above.

Now take the bottom right corner and fold it toward the center of the paper. The point of the corner should touch the center of the paper. Do the same thing with the upper right corner.

Step 2

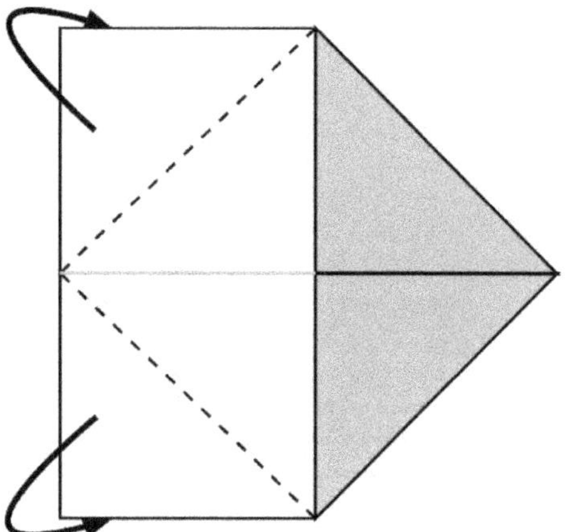

Now for this next move, you're going to do something similar to what you did in in **Step 1**, but you're going to do it in the *opposite* direction.

Take the bottom left corner and fold it toward the center of the square—but fold it *behind* the paper. Now do the same thing with the upper left corner

Step 3

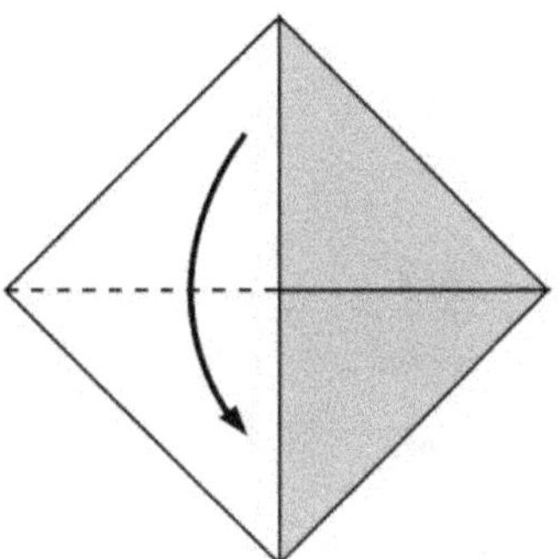

Fold the entire thing in half, bringing the top corner down to meet the bottom corner.

Step 4

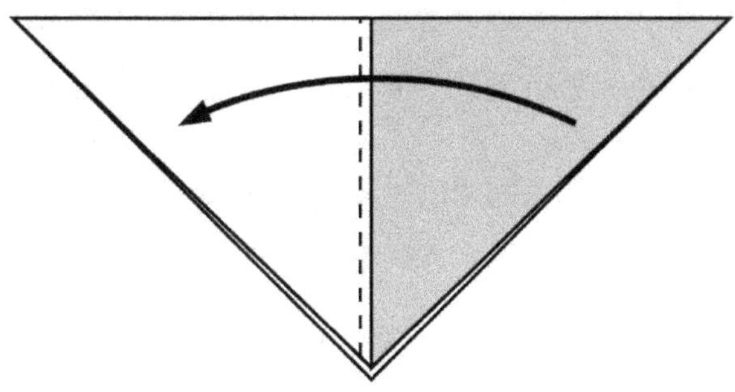

Fold it in half again, but this time fold from right to left.

Step 5

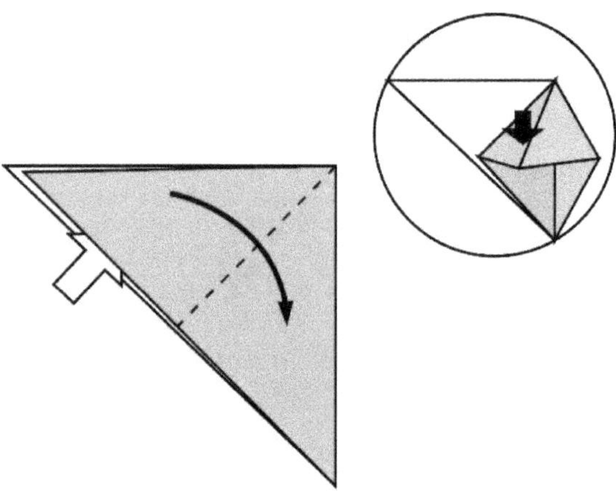

Now, this step here can get tricky. We now have two flaps. A top flap and a bottom flap. Notice the white arrow in the picture? This is where the top flap is. Take the top flap and open it, creasing the left and right sides so you can fold the top left corner to the bottom corner.

If you are still finding it difficult, grab the top part of the flap from where the dotted line starts on the left. You then want to pull it horizontally, across over to the right to get the flap to open up and fold over like the picture below.

Step 6

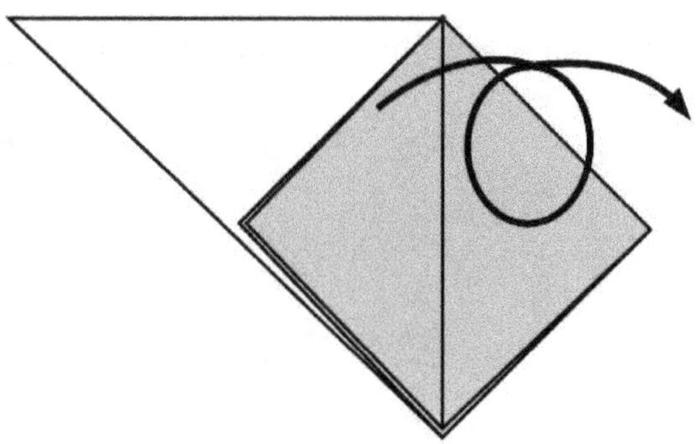

Now turn the paper over.

Step 7

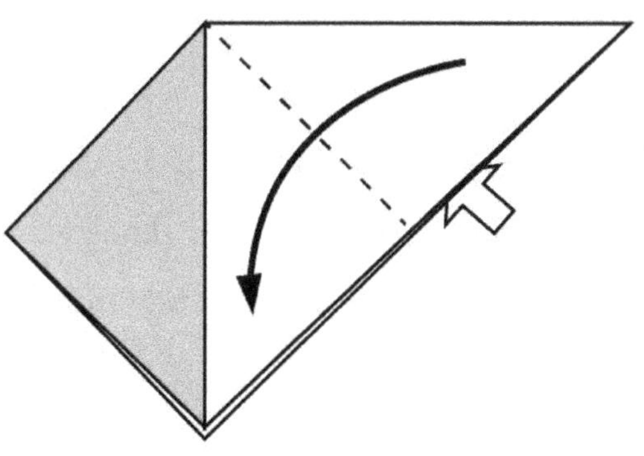

Here, we are going to repeat **Step 5**. Remember, this is the tricky one again. We're not folding the top right corner to the bottom corner. We are opening the flap from the start of the dotted line and pulling it over to the left corner. Read Step 5 again if you are having trouble. You should now have a pretty little square like the picture below.

Step 8

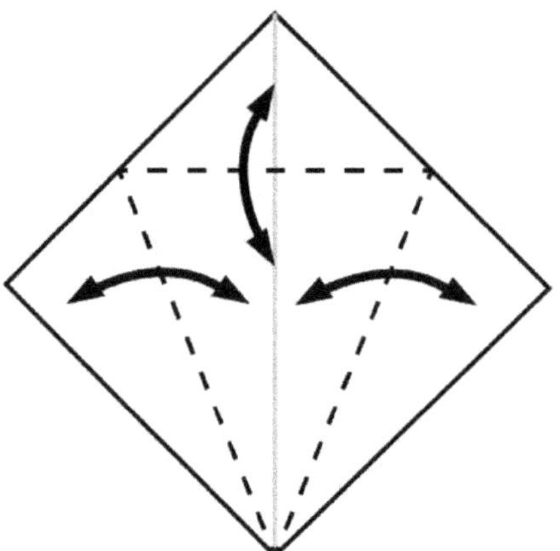

Take both left and right sides of the top layer and fold them in to meet at the middle, then unfold them. We then, want to fold the top corner down like in the picture above and unfold it. This step is preparation for what comes next.

Step 9

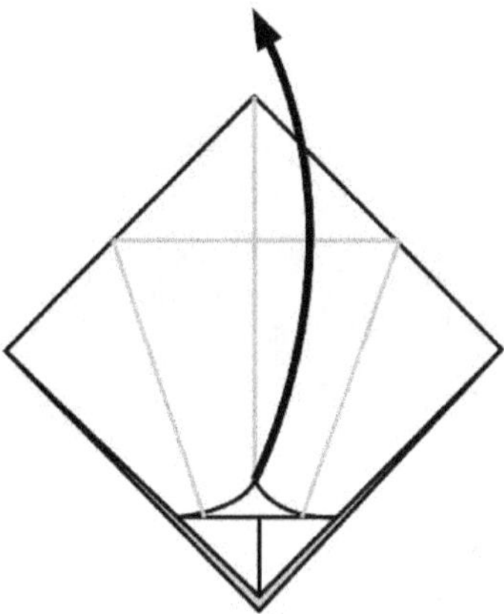

Open the flap upwards. You're going to make what's known as a petal fold. As the flap opens up, you want the bottom corner to meet the top corner and you should notice the flap to open up like a kite shape. You then want to flatten the left and right sides with the top corner so it is now smooth.

Step 10

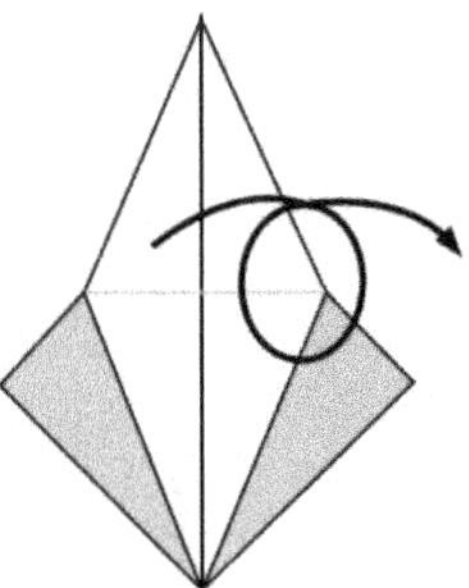

Once you have opened the flap and flattened it into a kite-looking shape, flip the paper over.

Step 11

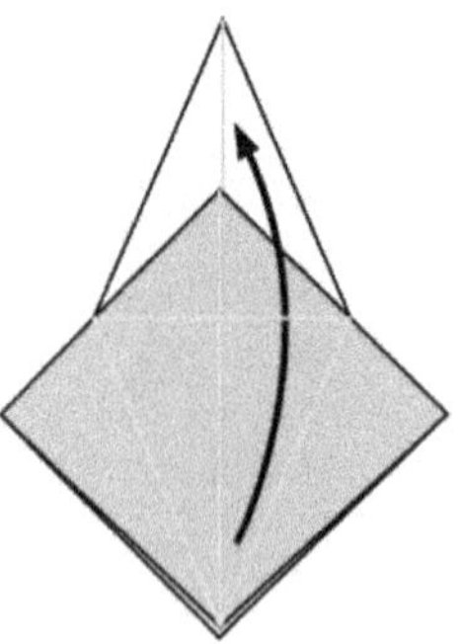

You're going to make the same petal fold on this side, too. So, you will be repeating **Step 9**. Take the top flap and pull it upwards to the top corner as pictured in the drawing above and flatten everything out.

Step 12

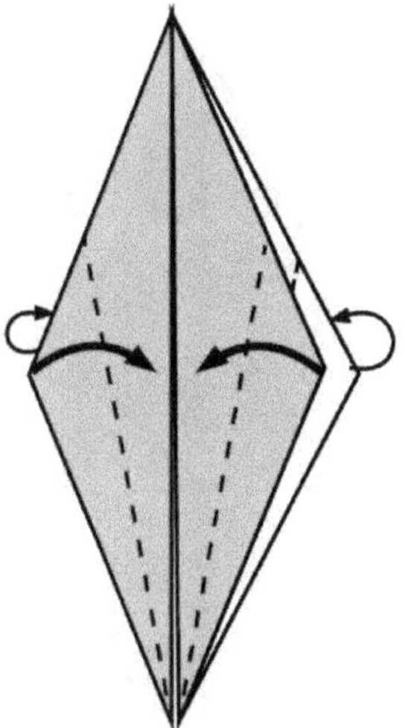

Your paper now looks like this. Congratulations! That part was hard!

Take the left and right corners of the top layer and fold toward the center of the piece. Not all the way to the center, but very close. Do this for the right and left sides.

Flip over and do the exact same thing for the other left and right corners. You should now have an even skinnier kite-looking shape.

Step 13

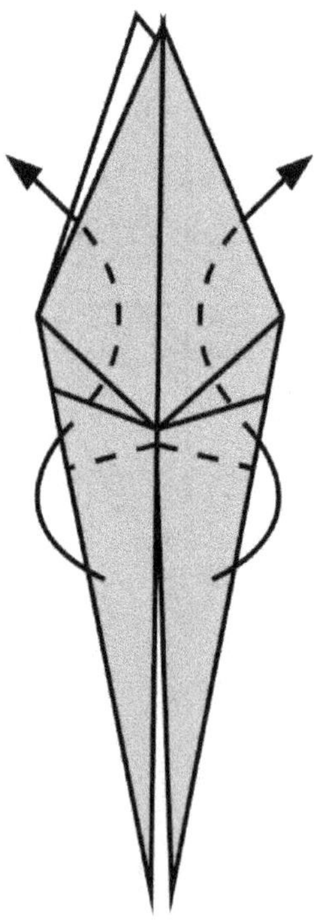

In this step, you're going to make two outside reverse folds with the flaps that are facing you. One will be for the head of the crane and the other will be for the tail of the crane. When you are done, the figure should resemble the drawing in **Step 14**.

Step 14

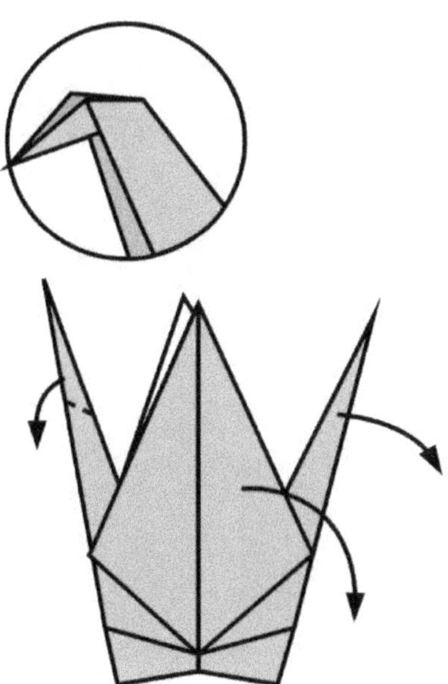

Firstly, flip the paper over. As you can see, everything is pointing up. We need to make our crane look like a crane! The two big flaps opposite each other are the crane's wings. Following the direction of the arrows in the drawing, pull the wings down slightly so that they're even with the floor.

On the right and left side of the drawing, you'll see the tail and head of your crane. Gently pull down the head and tail, but only slightly. You don't want them to be level with the crane's wings. You want the head and tail to stick up a bit.

On the head, you're going to do another outside reverse fold to give the crane a beak.

Step 15

The bird of happiness

Your crane, the bird of happiness, is now complete!

Final Words

I want to thank you for taking the time to make your way through my book. I hope it has given you a good introduction to the ancient art of origami, and that it has made you hungry to seek out more.

Before I go, I thought you might be interested in learning just a little about the man who made origami famous. Although no one persona can be said to have invented origami, one person did make origami popular in our time: Akira Yoshizawa.

Akira Yoshizawa was born in 1911. When he was only 13 years old, he moved to Tokyo to take a job in a factory. When he was in his early 20s, he was promoted to a new position that required him to train new workers. As a child, he had learned origami from his mother. He now taught it to his co-workers to help them understand their machines and how they worked.

During World War II, Akira Yoshizawa got sick and had to spend a long time in a hospital. He made origami models to cheer up the other sick patients.

By now, he was becoming famous for his beautiful origami. In 1951, a Japanese magazine asked him to fold some models for an article about origami. He did, and suddenly he became even more famous. He eventually published 18 books about origami.

Akira Yoshizawa's incredible skill allowed him to travel the world and get people interested in origami. The Japanese government asked him to be a special ambassador, and in 1983 named him to the Order of the Rising Sun, one of the highest honors for a citizen of Japan.

He died in 2005, when he was 94.

One of the most amazing things about Akira Yoshizawa is that he was a self-taught origami artist. And by that, I mean that he didn't just follow other people's designs—he made up entirely new designs of his own. His designs were complicated and beautiful and were shown in art galleries around the world. It is said that he created over 50,000 different origami models during his life.

He never used scissors or glue when creating his origami designs. One thing he did do, though, was create a new way of folding. It is called wet-folding, which means that the paper is dampened slightly before making a fold. Wet-folding allows the paper to be folded and bent more easily, and this means that the finished models have a rounder appearance and look more like sculpture. This was something entirely new in origami. No one had ever done it before. By the way, wet-folding requires thicker paper than traditional origami. Regular origami paper is usually very thin and will tear if wet-folding is tried.

I just wanted you to know a little about Akira Yoshizawa. He is the main reason that origami started to become popular in America after World War II. A lot of people never would have heard of origami had it not been for Akira Yoshizawa.

The world is a beautiful place. Sometimes, we get so busy that we miss it. Origami has allowed me to be still and to focus on the beauty of the world and all the things in it. The simplicity of this art is soothing to me, and I hope it has been—and will continue to be—for you, too.

But most of all, I hope you have fun!

If you enjoyed this book, I would greatly appreciate it if you left me a kind review on Amazon. I would love to hear your thoughts on my book and it really helps me to continue creating high quality books in the future.